EXPERIENCING
SAME-SEX MARRIAGE

This book is part of the Peter Lang Media and Communication list.
Every volume is peer reviewed and meets
the highest quality standards for content and production.

PETER LANG
New York • Washington, D.C./Baltimore • Bern
Frankfurt • Berlin • Brussels • Vienna • Oxford

PAMELA J. LANNUTTI

EXPERIENCING SAME-SEX MARRIAGE

Individuals, Couples, and Social Networks

PETER LANG
New York • Washington, D.C./Baltimore • Bern
Frankfurt • Berlin • Brussels • Vienna • Oxford

Library of Congress Cataloging-in-Publication Data
Lannutti, Pamela J.
Experiencing same-sex marriage: individuals, couples,
and social networks / Pamela J. Lannutti.
pages cm
Includes bibliographical references and index.
1. Same-sex marriage. 2. Interpersonal communication.
3. Sexual minorities—Social networks. I. Title.
HQ1033.L36   306.84'8—dc23   2013038202
ISBN 978-1-4331-2102-9 (hardcover)
ISBN 978-1-4539-1252-2 (e-book)

Bibliographic information published by **Die Deutsche Nationalbibliothek**.
Die Deutsche Nationalbibliothek lists this publication in the "Deutsche
Nationalbibliografie"; detailed bibliographic data is available
on the Internet at http://dnb.d-nb.de/.

The paper in this book meets the guidelines for permanence and durability
of the Committee on Production Guidelines for Book Longevity
of the Council of Library Resources.

© 2014 Peter Lang Publishing, Inc., New York
29 Broadway, 18th floor, New York, NY 10006
www.peterlang.com

Printed in Germany

Contents

Acknowledgments

I am grateful to those who have supported, encouraged, and assisted me in my research examining same-sex marriage over the past decade and have helped to make this book possible. First, I am grateful to the hundreds of GLBT people and same-sex couples who were graciously willing to share their time and experiences with me as I collected data over the years. I have always drawn inspiration and motivation for my research from teaching, so I am also grateful for my students at La Salle University and Boston College for the influence they have had on my same-sex marriage research. I am especially grateful for my former students who served as assistants on research discussed in this book: Leslie and Tara Abbott, Amanda Denes, and Maddie Redlick.

I have received inspiration and encouragement from many dear friends. Love and encouragement from Candice Costa and Stephanie Hunt have meant more to me than they know. Marie Butler, Rebecca Wingfield, Diane O'Connell, Carol Morris O'Connell, Amy Lipman, Sarah Goldman and Maria Grigoriadis have served as willing sounding boards and occasionally unwilling examples in my presentations and teaching. I am blessed to have friends within the Communication field who have been encouraging of my work, especially Jennifer Bevan, Leah Bryant, Megan Dillow, Ashley Duggan, Bonnie Jefferson, John Jordan, Kenny Lachlan Melanie Laliker, Jessica Moore, Chuck Morris, Archana Pathak, Beth Suter, and the MVCA. I am grateful to Paul Achter, Erin Sahlstein, and Kathryn Greene for inviting me to their campuses to present my work on same-sex marriage and providing me with encouragement and important feedback. I am grateful to Jennifer Monahan for teaching me how to be a scholar. I could not have completed much of the research discussed in this book without Dale Herbeck's friendship, wonderful department chairmanship, and championing of my work. Lynne Texter encouraged the beginning of my academic career as my undergraduate advisor and now serves as my ultra-supportive department chair in the Department of Communication at La Salle University. I am grateful to Lynne and my La Salle University colleagues for their support. I am especially thankful for the friendship, feedback, advice, encouragement, and motivation provided by Sandra Faulkner. It's a wonderful thing to have a friend that has supported you unconditionally (albiet with a healthy dose of mocking!) for over 20 years, and therefore I am so thankful that I met the Elena Strauman on the first day of college and that we have been able to share each step in our academic journies.

My work on same-sex marriage has been improved through the feedback and encouragement of editors, reviewers and colleagues. I am especially grateful to Leslie Baxter, Jerry Bigner, John De Cecco, Pearl Dykstra, Adam Fingerhut, Paz Galupo, Paul Mongeau, Sandra Petronio, Ellen D.B. Riggle, Sharon Scales Rostosky, and Mary Claire Morr Serewicz. Special thanks to my editor at Peter Lang, Mary Savigar.

I am very appreciative of the love and support of my family. Thank you to my parents, Paul and Marie Lannutti, and my brother and sister-in-law, Anthony and Kelly Lannutti, for their love and support. Special thanks to my niece, Juli, and my nephew, Ethan, for making sure I had fun and laughter breaks as I wrote this book. Frankie and Elvis have literally stayed by my side as I worked on this project. I am extremely grateful to Kellie Cochran for her love, encouragement, support, proofreading, formatting skills, and enduring patience!

Portions of the material in this book have appeared in my previous articles. Portions of Chapter 2 appeared in Lannutti (2005), "For better or worse: Exploring the meanings of same-sex marriage within the lesbian, gay, bisexual, and transgendered community," *Journal of Social and Personal Relationships*, 22, 5–18, SAGE Publications and Lannutti (2007a), "The influence of same-sex marriage on the understanding of same-sex relationships," *Journal of Homosexuality*, 53, 135–151, The Haworth Press. Portions of Chapter 3 appeared in Lannutti (2008), "Attractions and obstacles while considering legally recognized same-sex marriage," *Journal of GLBT Family Studies*, 4, 245–264, The Haworth Press. Portions of Chapter 4 appeared as Lannutti (2013), "Same-sex marriage and privacy management: Examining couples' communication with family members," *Journal of Family Communication*, 13, 60–75, Taylor and Francis. Portions of Chapter 5 appeared as Lannutti (2007b), "'This is not a lesbian wedding': Examining same-sex marriage and bisexual-lesbian couples," *Journal of Bisexuality*, 3–4, 239–260, The Haworth Press and Lannutti (2011), "Security, recognition, and misgivings: Exploring older same-sex couples' experiences of legally recognized same-sex marriage," *Journal of Social and Personal Relationships*, 28, 64–82, SAGE Publications. Portions of Chapter 6 appeared as Lannutti (2011b), "Examining communication about marriage amendments: Same-sex couples and their extended social networks," *Journal of Social Issues, 67,* 264–281, Wiley.

・ C H A P T E R   O N E ・

Introduction

lthought members of the gay, lesbian, bisexual, and transgender
(GLBT) community in the United States may be thought of by
many as leading untradiational lifestyles, the community does have
traditions. One such tradition is that the GLBT pride parade is lead by the
raucous Dykes on Bikes contingent in any given community. The Boston
GLBT Pride parade in June 2004 started off in the traditional way: the
waiting crowds lining the city streets and waving rainbow flags cheered as
the celebratory sounds of roaring motorcycles approached them. The riders
were rolling up the street with one bike leading the pack. The roars of the
motorcycles were deafening, but the sight of the leading rider was causing
the crowd's cheer to rise above the noise of the bikes. The woman driving
that first motorcycle smiled broadly, as did the passenger of the bike's
sidecar: another woman holding a "Just Married!" sign and the couple's
young child. That lead motorcycle didn't just signal the beginning of that
year's Pride parade, it signaled the beginning of a new relatonal context for
GLBT people, same-sex couples, and their social networks.

When those crowds were gathered in Boston for GBLT pride in June
2004, legally recognized same-sex marriages in the United States had only
been available since the previous month and were only available in Massachusetts. Same-sex marriage was recognized in Massachusetts when on
November 18, 2003, the Massachusetts Supreme Judicial Court (SJC) de-
clared that it could find no "constitutionally adequate reason for denying
civil marriage to same-sex couples," and ordered the state to begin issuing
marriage licenses to same-sex couples after a 180-day stay period
(*Goodridge v. Dept. of Public Health*, 2003). The SJC decision marked a turning point in the fight for and against same-sex marriage that had been oc-
curring across the United States for nearly a decade (Alderson & Lahey,
2004; Pinello, 2006). Although some American states and municipalities had
been legally issuing same-sex couples civil protection for several years (see
Pinello, 2006, and *Marriage*, n.d., for reviews), the Massachusetts SJC decision marked the first time that American same-sex partners would be legally granted the same civil marriage protections as heterosexual couples.

At the time this book was written, Massachusetts had been joined in recognizing same-sex sex marriage by 13 other U.S. states and the capitol: Connecticut (2008), Iowa (2009), Vermont (2009), Washington, D.C. (2009), New Hampshire (2010), New York (2011), Maine (2012), Maryland (2012), Washington (2012), Minnesota (2013), Delaware (2013), Rhode Island (2013), and New Jersey (2013). In California, same-sex marriage was recognized for a period before a ballot measure known as Proposition 8 amended the state constitution to define marriage as a union between one man and one woman. However, after a ruling by the Supreme Court of the United States in June 2013, California began issuing marriage licenses to same-sex couples again. While same-sex marriage recognition in the U.S. expanded, there was also a movement in other parts of the country to limit relationship recognition for same-sex couples. In the United States, 38 states had either amended their state constitutions or passed legislation to prohibit the legal recognition of same-sex marriage (see *Marriage*, n.d.). For U.S. same-sex couples and their marriage recognition status, the old real estate motto "location, location, location" has a unique and important meaning. For example, a southeastern Pennsylvania same-sex couple who wants to live in a state where they can have a legal marriage can drive for just 15 minutes to Wilmington, Delaware, and start looking for a home. But, if one of the partners still works in Pennsylvania, that Pennsylvania employer is not legally obligated to provide spousal benefits for the couple. And, although Delaware recognized the couple's marriage, until Supreme Court rulings on June 26, 2013, the federal government did not. Thus, where a same-sex couple lives has a huge impact on the kinds of rights and protections they can have for their relationship.

The United States is not the only country with legal recognition for same-sex marriage in all or parts of the country. At the time this book was written, 16 countries had nationwide recognition for same-sex marriage (Argentina, Belgium, Brazil, Canada, Denmark, Great Britain, Iceland, the Netherlands, Norway, Portugal, Spain, South Africa, Sweden, Uruguay, New Zealand, and France). Across the globe, the battle for and against legally recognized same-sex marriage continues. While there has been an increase in recognition for same-sex marriage, there have also been victories for those wishing to ban same-sex marriage. Furthermore, same-sex sexual relations still remain illegal in many nations across the globe. Undoubtedly, by the time you read this book, there will have been further developments regarding the legal recognition of same-sex marriage.

In addition to legislation and legal cases, the dynamic and rapidly changing battle for and against legally recognized same-sex marriage has produced hours of political debates, hundreds of public protests, countless TV and radio talk show discussions, widely spread social media campaigns, numerous comedy skits and even a few celebrity weddings. But what has often been lost in all of the same-sex marriage hoopla has been a focus on the experiences of people most affected by the battle for and against legally recognized same-sex marriage: GLBT people, same-sex couples, and their families and friends (referred to as their "social networks"). The purpose of this book is to provide an understanding of how the legal and cultural debates and advances and limitations on same-sex marriage are experienced by GLBT people, same-sex couples, and their social networks. To do so, this book examines experiences of same-sex marriage through the lens of the social scientific study of relationships. In particular, this book is based on a Communication Studies perspective on personal relationships, and therefore emphasizes Communication concepts and theories relevant to the understanding of same-sex marriage experiences. Further, given the dynamic nature of the battle for and against legally recognized same-sex marriage in the United States and the differences in legal status for same-sex couples across the U.S., this book focuses on the experiences of same-sex marriage in the U.S. only.

Same-sex Marriage Experiences through a Communication Studies Lens

The study of communication is a diverse field with interdisciplinary roots and connections, but the common thread throughout the study of communication is a focus on messages and message processes. The study of communication in personal relationships focuses on how people's interactions shape and are shaped by their relationship to one another. Some central tenants of the study of communication in personal relationships are key to understanding the experiences of same-sex marriage presented in this book.

First, it is important to understand that communication is central to relationships. As Dindia (2003, p. 1) explains, "To maintain a relationship, partners must communicate with one another. Conversely, as long as people communicate, they have a relationship...the quality of a relationship is primarily determined by the quality of the communication in the relationship." Thus, to understand a personal relationship, such as a marriage, it is important to understand the communication that takes place within the relationship. Communication scholars have argued that interactions, especially our everyday interactions, are central to building and maintaining not only our social worlds, but also our identities and understanding of self (see Tracy, 2002, for review).

A second tenant of communication in personal relationships relevant to understanding same-sex marriage experiences is the idea that communication shapes perceptions, and perceptions shape our communication. Communication influences our perceptions of our selves. As we process, evaluate, and compare ourselves to the messages about us from others' (either those we know personally or the generalized "other" of society), we build and shift our understandings of ourselves. Therefore, we can expect that GLBT people and their friends and family will have their self-concepts and self-evaluations impacted by messages about same-sex marriage from a variety of sources. People's communication regarding same-sex marriage will be affected by their own self-concepts and self-evaluations.

Communication influences our perceptions of others and our relationships with others. Through interacting with other people and observing them interact with each other, we develop our understandings of those around us and our relationships with them. Thus, we can expect that people's understanding of their partners, friends, family members, and their relationships with these people will be affected by messages related to same-sex marriage. Further, people's interactions regarding same-sex marriage will be influenced by the ways they perceive those with whom they are interacting and their relationship with them.

The third tenant of the study of communication in personal relationships that is key to understanding experiences of same-sex marriage is that communication occurs within a context, and that communication is both affected by and affects that context. The context for communication is complex, and can be a combination of the relational, cultural, sociological, psychological, temporal, and physical environments in which the interactions take place. Therefore, when examining an interaction about same-sex marriage, it is important to remember the many layers of context that shape that interaction. I argue that the complexities of the battles for and against same-sex marriage experienced by GLBT people, same-sex couples, and their social networks form a new and influential context for their relational lives. Further, interactions among people influence the context for that interaction and future interactions. As such, communication among GLBT people, same-sex couples and their social network members serve to shape the environment of their interactions with one another and others.

The centrality of communication to personal relationships and the reciprocal relationships between communication and perceptions and communication and context form the theoretical foundation for the exploration of same-sex marriage experiences in this book. Throughout the book, specific theories of communication in personal relationships are also used to examine the same-sex marriage experiences of GLBT people, same-sex couples, and their social networks.

Looking Ahead in This Book

This book combines the work of many scholars with my own research on same-sex marriage experiences. My own investigations into the same-sex marriage experiences of GLBT people, same-sex couples, and their social networks discussed in this book began in 2003 after the Massachusetts Supreme Judicial Court announced its decision to allow same-sex marriages in the state and continued for the next decade. While specific methodological approaches used in my own studies are detailed throughout the book, one common aspect of these research studies is that they rely on qualitative data. A qualitative approach was used for two primary reasons. First, my research studies represented in this book are some of the first studies of same-sex marriage in America from a communication perspective. As such, it was important to build a descriptive foundation of the same-sex marriage experiences of GLBT people, same-sex couples and their social networks. Second, the research studies were conducted to place an emphasis on the detailed descriptions of their experiences as provided by participants. Because legally recognized same-sex marriage in the U.S. is new and its status changes so rapidly, I wanted to provide a detailed view into the experiences and communication of those most affected by this societal change as they described it in their own words. A qualitative data collection approach allows me to capture the language of the participants, adding an additional nuance to our understanding of their experiences. This book includes many quotes directly from people who participated in my research studies. Names associated with quotes from people who participated in my studies are pseudonyms.

In the chapters that follow, I provide a view into the same-sex marriage experiences of U.S. GLBT people, same-sex couples, and their social networks. The next chapter of this book discusses how legally recognized same-sex marriage can be understood as a new relational context for GLBT individuals, same-sex couples, and their social networks. The chapter includes a discussion of my research examining how GLBT individuals in Massachusetts assigned meaning to legally recognized same-sex marriage when it was first introduced in the state and how the option to legally marry has influenced GLBT individuals' perceptions of their romantic relationships and romantic relationships in general.

The third chapter examines same-sex couples' decision-making process as they face the issue of whether to marry or not. Most same-sex couples who marry in the early period of the legal recognition of marriage in their location have been in a committed romantic relationship for a significant period of time. As such, they have already established means of communicating their commitment to each other and their social networks. The chapter includes a discussion of my research examining the attractions and obstacles to getting married reported by married and engaged same-sex couples, as well as my research on the experiences of established same-sex couples who have the option for legally recognized marriage in their locations but choose to not marry.

One of the most common obstacles mentioned by same-sex couples as they deliberate about whether to marry or not is opposition to their marriage by family-of-origin members. Chapter four focuses on the interactions between same-sex couples and members of their families-of-origin regarding same-sex marriage. The chapter also includes a discussion of same-sex marriage and families headed by same-sex couples.

Although the people commonly refer to the "GLBT" community when discussing same-sex marriage, the uniqueness of the experiences of certain segments of the community is often overlooked. As a result, the value of the diversity of experiences related to same-sex marriage within the community is often lost or diminished. Chapter five focuses on research about the same-sex marriage experiences of some understudied members of the GLBT community. More specifically, chapter five focuses on the same-sex marriage-related experiences of bisexual-lesbian couples in more detail. The chapter also includes a discussion of the ways that older same-sex couples assign meaning to legally recognized same-sex marriage with a unique historical perspective.

Chapter two makes the argument that legally recognized same-sex marriage can be understood as a new relational context for GLBT individuals, same-sex couples, and their social networks. This new relational context has implications for the relational experiences of those who have the option to legally marry and those who do not. Chapter six will focus on the experiences of GLBT individuals, same-sex couples, and their social network members in U.S. locations that have enacted legislation banning legal recognition for same-sex marriage.

Finally, chapter seven offers an overview of the implications of legally recognized same-sex marriage for the relational experiences of GLBT individuals, same-sex couples, and their social networks. The chapter discusses limitations of the research on same-sex marriage experiences presented in this book and suggests directions for future research.

Legally Recognized Same-sex Marriage as a New Relational Context

On June 6, 2013, the PEW Research Center for the People and the Press released new data about American attitudes toward legally recognized same-sex marriage (PEW Research Center, 2013). The poll revealed that the number of Americans who support same-sex marriage reached beyond 50% for the first time since PEW began polling about the issue in 2003 (PEW Reseach Center, 2013). According to PEW's (2013) study, 72% of Americans surveyed believed that legal recognition of same-sex marriage was inevitable. 72% is a large percentage, especially when you consider that PEW's poll in 2004 indicated that only 59% of Americans surveyed believed that legal recognition of same-sex marriage was inevitable. These poll results are indicative of a shift in American culture when it comes to same-sex marriage. The poll shows how rapidly public opinion about the place of same-sex marriage in American life has changed from 2004 when Massachusetts became the first state to allow same-sex couples to legally wed to nearly a decade later when same-sex couples could wed in 13 states and D.C. While public opinion polls like those produced by PEW can show us a picture of large opinion shifts and trends, they cannot tell us much about how GLBT people, same-sex couples, and their social networks are affected by them. This chapter explores how legally recognized same-sex marriage forms a new relational context for GLBT people, same-sex couples, and their social networks and how that context affects their perceptions and relationships.

To better understand experiences of same-sex marriage in the U.S., I could say it is important to start at the beginning and look back to the time when same-sex marriage was first available to U.S. couples. But, when it comes to same-sex marriage, the U.S. is stuck in a kind of legal recognition limbo. As I write this book, same-sex couples in the U.S. have been able to legally marry in some states for a decade and public opinion has shifted such that most American's support legal same-sex marriage and believe same-sex marriage recognition in the U.S. to be inevitable (PEW Research, 2013). The Supreme Court of the United States ruled in June 2013 that the Defense of Marriage Act (DOMA), which defined marriage as a union between one man and one woman, was unconstitutional, thus allowing same-sex couples who are married in their state to have that marriage recognized by the federal government as well (*United States v. Windsor*, 2013). Yet, thousands of same-sex couple across the U.S. still live in a state that has either banned same-sex marriage and/or refuses to recognize same-sex marriages from states that do offer legal marriages to same-sex couples. Therefore, the advent of legally recognized same-sex marriage is in the past for some couples but still in the future for others.

Still, I argue that the battle for and against same-sex marriage and the introduction of legal marriage and marriage bans across the U.S. all contribute to a new relational context for American same-sex couples regardless of location. Whether an American same-sex couple can marry where they reside or not, the availability of same-sex marriage in some states, the moves to ban same-sex marriage in other states, and the national debate about same-sex marriage affects their perceptions, communication, and relationships. As discussed earlier, there is a recriporocal relationship between context and the communication we have with one another. This communication is also interdependent with our understanding of our selves and our relationships. To better understand experiences of same-sex marriage, this chapter presents research I conducted examining how the introduction of same-sex marriage and the related battle for and against legal recognition for same-sex couples affect the meaning making and relationships of GLBT people and same-sex couples.

Perceptions and Experiences of the Introduction of Same-sex Marriage in the U.S.

When the Massachusetts Supreme Judicial Court (SJC) announced their decision in *Goodridge v. Department of Public Health*, they ordered the state to begin issuing marriage licenses to same-sex couples after a 180-day stay period (*Goodridge v. Dept. of Public Health*, 2003). As a result, GLBT people in Massachusetts knew that legally recognized marriage was about to begin in the near future, but had time before anyone actually got married to contemplate this new opportunity for relationship recognition. During the 180-day stay period after the SJC ruling but before marriages began, I had the opportunity to examine the ways that GLBT people were making sense of the impending legalization of same-sex marriage in Massachusetts (see Lannutti, 2005, and Lannutti, 2007a).[1] Although I had originally planned to include only GLBT people who lived in Massachusetts in the sample for the study, the snowball sampling method that I used to gather the sample spread to GLBT people nationwide. A total of 288 GLBT people participated in the study (166 participants resided in Massachusetts, and 122 resided in another part of the U.S.).[2] Thus, the perspectives represented in the study support the idea that first legal recognition of same-sex marriage in the U.S. affected GLBT people who did and did not live in the state issuing the marriage licenses. In particular, I wanted to examine two things. First, I wanted to learn how GLBT people thought that legally recognized same-sex marriage would affect the GLBT community. Second, I wanted to learn how the impending possibility of legally recognized same-sex marriage was affecting GLBT peoples' perceptions of their own romantic relationship and romantic relationships in general.

I chose to focus my investigation, in part, upon the impact of legally recognized same-sex marriage on the GLBT community because of the unique relationships among GLBT individuals, same-sex couples and the GLBT community. The conceptualization of the GLBT "community" has been controversial, with the "community" having been described as existing on many planes ranging from a close group of friends to inhabitants of a shared gay ghetto to a largely imagined group of individuals who have same-sex desire in common (Holt, 2011; Woolwine, 2000). Although different-sex couples also experience relational processes within a broader social context (Parks & Eggert, 1991), Stearns and Sabini (1997) point out that same-sex couples often experience a unique type of community influence on their relational processes because same-sex couples are part of a minority group defined by relational and sexual preference. Many same-sex couples often find acceptance only within the GLBT community, rely on community organizations for specialized resources, and/or negotiate their separateness from the community due to the pressures of heterosexism (sometimes internalized) or to protect their relationship (Meyer, 1990; Peplau & Cochran, 1981; Stearns & Sabini, 1997). As such, the links between same-sex couples and the GLBT community have been shown to be complex and participation in the community from couples and individuals varied (Holt, 2011). Yet, the potential implications of legally recognized same-sex marriage were likely to be so widespread that it could have reshaped important dynamics of the relationship among the GLBT community, GLBT individuals, and same-sex couples.

The study revealed that GLBT individuals' expectations about the ways that legally recognized same-sex marriage would affect them, their relationships, and the GLBT community were complex. Yet, there was on overarching theme that was mentioned by nearly every one of the GLBT people who participated in the study. Nearly every person indicated that the legal recognition of same-sex marriage represented an important type of legal equality for GLBT people, and this was seen as affecting the GLBT community for the better.

As they described legal equality through same-sex marriage, GLBT people who participated in the study mentioned three things: first-class citizenship, financial benefits, and family security. First-class citizenship reflected the participants' beliefs that the legal recognition of same-sex marriage marks the end of differing legal protections and treatment for GLBT and heterosexual American citizens. One person expressed the end of "second class citizenship," "We now have the same rights as everybody else. They can't say we are second class or not as worthy of legal rights as straights anymore." Another stated, "This finally makes us real American citizens. It shows that we are Americans and being married is part of our fundamental American rights." So strong was some participants' view of same-sex marriage as a vehicle for first-class citizenship that they rejected the relational aspects of marriage and instead defined marriage in legal terms only. For example, one person stated:

> Having same-sex marriage, and calling it marriage especially, makes the discussion about gay relationships a legal one, not a religious or moral issue. This shows everyone that we are citizens, we pay taxes, and we have to be treated the same as everybody else. So, this isn't about marriage, it's about equal rights.

GLBT people also mentioned the financial benefits of same-sex marriage. As one person said, "Having the right to get married means that same-sex couples can now get the tax breaks and other financial perks, such as getting to share property, of being married." Many GLBT people thought of the financial benefits of legal equality in terms of health and insurance benefits. For example, "Now couples will be able to share health insurance, and that's really important, especially to older couples or when one partner can't work."

GLBT individuals also discussed same-sex marriage as a means for increased security for GLBT families. One person's statement reflected many individuals' concerns for same-sex couples with children,

> Being able to get married will help couples who have children or want to have children. It should help in adoptions a lot if the couple can say they are married. It will make sure all GLBT families are legally protected.

Others thought ahead to protection of families in times of crisis. For example,

> Being able to get married means that I will be able to take care of my partner, like making medical or other types of decisions for him, if something horrible happens or when we are older because everyone will have to recognize me as his partner.

While nearly all of the GLBT people who participated in the study agreed that same-sex marriage should be understood, at least in part, as a way of gaining legal equality for GLBT people in the United States, legal equality was not the only way in which participants understood same-sex marriage. Understanding of same-sex marriage and its expected effects on the GLBT community went beyond legal equality and were revealed in contradictory expectations about same-sex marriage and how it would affect the GLBT community, the relationship between the GLBT community and non-GLBT community members, and couples.

Dialectical Tensions and Expectations of Same-sex Marriage

One prominent theoretical perspective in the study of relationships through a Communication Studies lens derives from Baxter and Montgomery's (1996) theory of relational dialectics. Baxter and Montgomery (1996) described relational dynamics and communication as dialectical processes in which people experience simultaneously contradictory forces. These forces, or dialectics, drive changes in relationships and are both affected by and affect communication between relational partners. The dialectics within a relationship are interdependent with each other and the context in which the communication takes place (Baxter, 2011; Baxter & Montgomery, 1996). Therefore, dialectics should be examined not only at the dyadic level, but at the larger societal level as well.

As I tried to understand how GLBT people were making sense of the impending advent of legally recognized same-sex marriage in Massachusetts, I found it helpful to apply a dialectical perspective to the responses I received from my participants. Within the GLBT individual responses about their expectations of same-sex marriage, I found three dialectical themes at three interconnected levels: the GLBT community, between the GLBT community and non-GLBT community members, and couples.

GLBT community. The first dialectical theme that emerged from the responses of GLBT people who participated in the study focused on same-sex marriages' possible effect on the GLBT community itself. GLBT people described their simultaneous and contradictory beliefs that same-sex marriage would make the community stronger and weaker. GLBT individuals' beliefs that same-sex marriage would make the GLBT community stronger centered around two ideas: validation and unification. First, GLBT people saw the legal recognition of same-sex marriage as extending beyond legal equality to creating a sense of validation for the community and its members. As one person stated, "Same-sex marriage is a wonderful thing for the GLBT community because it shows us that we matter and we are to be respected in our ways of loving and living our lives." Another wrote, "There is such joy in the community right now because of [same-sex marriage]. It's like the whole state is celebrating lesbian and gay relationships." Others expressed validation through their belief that same-sex marriage will serve to diminish internalized homophobia within the community. For example:

> Even though being gay is a lot better than it was 20 years ago, lots of members of our community still feel oppressed and have come to believe that they are worthless because they are queer. This marriage thing says it's really ok to be gay in a huge way and that should help to lessen the internalized homophobia going around. If we stop hating ourselves, we will be so much stronger as a group.

GLBT people also saw legally recognized same-sex marriage as strengthening the GLBT community through unification. For example, one person stated:

> What's important here isn't just that we finally have the legal right to marry, but that we as a community fought long and hard for this and have a real victory to hold on to. Even though we won in Massachusetts, the fight for equality is not over here or anywhere yet, but the community has really come together and is being strong together.

Other GLBT people saw unification not in political terms, but in terms of the dynamics of relationships within the community. For example:

> Gay marriage will help to tie partnered gay people to the community as a whole. Before, if you were in a long-term relationship, you sort of lost touch with the community because the community seemed to be for single people who were interested in hooking-up. This whole gay marriage thing shows that partnered people are welcome and needed in the community because the community wanted marriage as an option.

While same-sex marriage was understood as making the GLBT community stronger through validation and unification, GLBT people who participated in the study also espoused an opposing view that saw same-sex marriage weakening the GLBT community. Same-sex marriage was seen as potentially weakening the GLBT community through stigmatization and assimilation. The stigmatization associated with same-sex marriage in the present responses differs from that usually presented in studies of the GLBT community (e.g., DiPlacido, 1998), which describe the experience of being GLBT as setting one apart from the norms of mainstream/heterosexual society. Instead, the participants foresaw same-sex marriage as setting up a stigmatizing system *within* the GLBT community as getting married becomes the norm and remaining unmarried becomes stigmatized. As one person explained:

Same-sex marriage will set up marriage as the ultimate relational goal and make other ways of relating and loving invalid in the community. People will start to wonder what is wrong with you if you are in a good relationship and you don't get married, and will be disappointed in you if you say you just don't see marriage as something you want for your life.

Some people suggested that the stigma of not getting married will lead to non-married couples losing the GLBT community's support. For example, "I think that the same-sex marriage is a good thing, but that it will cause some trouble. I mean, the community isn't going to take a couple seriously unless they get married now." Another person predicted the stigma of not marrying will divide the GLBT community into two distinct groups:

I guess there will now be the 'haves' and the 'have-nots' when it comes to marriage. This will cause a split in the community because the married gays will look down on the non-married gays and the non-married gays will probably be seen as rebels or trouble-makers. At the very least, there will be a split because the married and non-married gays will want different things for the community and will not work together anymore.

Finally, other people expressed the idea of stigma and same-sex marriage as causing divides between gay men and lesbians and other members of the community. For example:

Same-sex marriage is great if you are gay or lesbian, but if you are bisexual this will just force you out of the 'GLBT' community more. I mean, gay and lesbian people will want a same-sex marriage now and if you are bi you might not want to do that, so you will be an outcast in a way because you won't be seen as worth having a relationship with anymore.

Another expressed concern about the transgender segment of the GLBT community:

I'm not sure where same-sex marriage leaves you if you are trans or genderqueer. There are issues of identity (psychologically and legally) that the trans community is facing that are glossed over when you think about same-sex marriage because it is so dependent on 'same-sex' which may or may not apply in relationships with a genderqueer or trans partner. It seems to me that married gay and lesbian couples are being seen as the 'right' kind of relationship, and that just makes the MTFs, FTMs, butches, bois, queers and everyone else who doesn't fall in a neat little box fit less and less into the so-called GLBT community.

In addition to stigmatization, GLBT people also expected same-sex marriage to weaken the GLBT community through a process of assimilation. They sensed that same-sex marriage may lead to the GLBT community losing its unique culture and instead move closer to what they saw as a straight status quo. Many mentioned the loss of difference when same-sex marriage is legally recognized. For example, "Having the same marriage rights as everybody else also means that we will become everybody else. We just won't be unique anymore." Others expressed the theme of assimilation by talking about how same-sex marriage will affect relational dynamics:

> Same-sex marriage might impose a cookie-cutter set of rules on our relationships. Gay and lesbian couples have been special in that we could have more fluid, and more realistic, relationships, but now that will change. The unique way we defined our relationships was one of the things that made the community so special, and I am sad to see that part of us go.

Another person agreed that a change in the way GLBT relationships are defined takes something away from the community:

> Legalization of same-sex marriages might lead us to take our relationships for granted. I mean, it's not a big deal anymore to stand-up for your relationship if you can get married. Before, it was a big deal to make a commitment and say you were 'married' to your partner because it meant you were brave and standing up for your relationship in the face of all that said you couldn't. Some of the bravery of being gay and out and together is gone now.

Finally, others saw the assimilation potential of same-sex marriage as weakening the GLBT community because same-sex marriage could be seen as a way of incorporating the norms of heterosexual relational culture. As one person explained, "Marriage itself is a fundamentally flawed institution. It's patriarchal and makes people think they own other people. Now, the GLBT community has bought into that." Another stated,

> I just think that same-sex marriage makes it look like all along we've wanted to be straight and that all the horrible things that happen in straight marriages, like abuse and divorce, are fine with us. We aren't as strong as a community because we aren't fighting against the mainstream now, we are wanting to be a part of it.

My study is not the first to identify GLBT concerns about legally recognized same-sex marriage and the dangers of internal stigmatization and assimilation to the GLBT community. Yep, Lovaas, and Elia (2003) compare the ideologies reflected in recent GLBT popular literature in which assimilationist writers claim same-sex marriage will improve the GLBT community while radical writers see same-sex marriage as the community's downfall. Some GLBT activists have argued that the fight for same-sex marriage has shifted the GLBT communities' social activism from a broader quest for equality to a too narrow and too assimilating focus on marriage which privileges only one perspective on valuable same-sex relationships (see Schulman, 2009; Sullivan, 2004; Wharton & Philips, 2004).

Interestingly, the GLBT people who participated in my study reflected both positions (that same-sex marriage will strengthen and weaken the GLBT community), but did so not by choosing one side or the other. Instead, they acknowledged both positions as part of their overall understanding of same-sex marriage. Thus, both sides of the dialectical tension, strengthening/weakening the GLBT community, simultaneously contribute to participants' understanding of legally recognized same-sex marriage as a context for their relationships and place in society.

Between the GLBT community and non-GLBT community members. Another dialectical theme that emerged from the GLBT individuals' understandings of legally recognized same-sex marriage concerns the relationship between the GLBT community and non-GLBT community members. GLBT people saw same-sex marriage as a tool for healing the relationship between those inside and outside the GLBT community. Yet, they simultaneously understood that same-sex marriage may be used by non-GLBT community members as a weapon to injure the GLBT community.

GLBT people expressed their beliefs that legally recognized same-sex marriage would help improve the relationship between the GLBT community and non-GLBT community members in several ways. Many looked at same-sex marriage as a beneficial public relations tool for the GLBT community that would lead to greater acceptance of the community by those outside the community. For example,

> Same-sex marriage won't just change the community, but the way the community is viewed by those outside of it. If straight people see that we want to get married, they will have to realize that the stereotypes of gays as promiscuous are wrong. Basically, same-sex marriage will help to reduce homophobia in the straight community.

Another person expressed a similar sentiment,

> Same-sex marriage will help to reduce the stress felt by sexual minorities because it will help reduce the misunderstanding and rejection that they feel from heterosexual people. Marriage makes relationships and families more visible and will make those outside the community question their ignorance.

In addition to helping to change non-GLBT community members' perceptions of the GLBT community, same-sex marriage was seen as a tool for improving GLBT/heterosexual relations by encouraging wider acceptance of GLBT relationships. For example, "Same-sex marriage makes our relationships really count. Straights can't ignore us anymore, and I think most of them will come to accept us better if they see that we are married just like they are." Another person put the idea of acceptance in more personal terms:

> It would be nice if marriage made straight people, in general, like gay people more, but I think it will really matter when you look at it in the smaller scale, like looking at families. If you get married, your straight family will be able to better accept and integrate your partner in the family because being married is something that is easier for them to understand and accept.

Thus, same-sex marriage was seen as a tool to heal perceived rifts between the GLBT community and non-GLBT community members by reducing homophobia and ignorance and increasing acceptance and integration of GLBT community members into the larger society.

While GLBT people who participated in the study saw the potential for same-sex marriage to improve the relationship between the GLBT community and those outside it, they also pointed out the potential for legally recognized same-sex marriage to be used as a weapon by a segment of mainstream society to hurt the GLBT community. Participants were wary of the potential scrutiny of the GLBT community that would accompany same-sex marriage:

> Same-sex marriage opens up our community to public scrutiny, especially from conservatives and the media. I mean, there has never been a gay divorce rate before and now it will be public knowledge when we break up and it will be reported the same way stats on straight divorce are, but in our case, these stats will be used as 'proof' that we shouldn't have been allowed to marry in the first place. It puts a lot of pressure on those getting married to stay together, and pressure on the whole community to make sure we don't add fuel to the fire.

Others expressed concern that same-sex marriage would force increases in GLBT visibility, and therefore, increase vulnerability for physical and verbal attack. For example,

> Same-sex marriage is probably really upsetting a lot of ignorant straight people out there. If you get married, everyone in your town will know you are a lesbian or gay couple, and in some places that could be like painting a target on your head.

Another participant's statement represents the hurt felt from anti-same-sex marriage campaigns:

> Same-sex marriage is opposed by a lot of the straight community and it has been really painful to hear everyone from politicians to church leaders to just plain people on the subway talk about how disgusting it is for GLBT people to get married or worse, how disgusting we are period. It's like the issue of same-sex marriage has given people free range to make homophobic and offensive statements anywhere and to anyone they please.

As with the other dialectical themes, participants understood the meaning of same-sex marriage and the relationship between the GLBT community and those outside of it as incorporating two opposing poles. On one hand, they saw same-sex marriage as a tool to heal the schism between the GLBT and "straight" community. On the other hand, they pointed to the ways in which same-sex marriage could be used as a tool by segments of "straight" society to injure the GLBT community.

Same-sex couples. GLBT people had contradictory, yet simultaneous views of same-sex marriage as a means for same-sex partnerships to become more serious and more fanciful. On one side, GLBT people expressed their belief that same-sex marriage will make same-sex couples take their relationships more seriously and strengthen same-sex partnerships in a variety of ways. For example, one person saw same-sex marriage as adding seriousness for those who marry as well as those who do not,

> Getting married will help couples feel closer to each other and will make their relationship stronger. Couples who don't get married right away will realize that they can work toward a serious relationship in the future because they have the option of getting married someday.

Others felt that same-sex marriage would make stronger relationships because the institutionalization of same-sex relationships creates a type of structural barrier to relational dissolution (Attridge, 1994; Johnson, 1982). For example,

> Marriage makes people take a relationship more seriously and realize that they need to work on it instead of just leaving when things get tough. Gay people will now have to look at their relationships as more stable and permanent because they are marriages.

Other responses linked stronger relationships to a stronger GLBT community as a result of same-sex marriage. For example,

> Being able to get married will make the whole community stronger and happier because people will be more supported in their relationships, but will also be held more accountable for them in the eyes of others. After all, we all want lesbian and gay marriages to work out.

While GLBT people saw same-sex marriage as resulting in more serious same-sex partnerships, they also expressed the opposite idea by suggesting that same-sex marriage might encourage more fanciful relationships. Many expressed concern that the excitement of having legally recognized marriage for the first time may lead same-sex couples to marry for the "wrong reasons." For example,

> Same-sex marriage could be a problem for couples and the whole community if people get married for the wrong reasons. Like, if people marry just because they can now, or because it seems like the cool thing to do if you are gay or lesbian now.

Another person offered, "Having the ability to get married is great, but not if people get married without thinking long and hard about the lifetime commitment they are making. I think getting married is going to be a fad for a while." Others were concerned that same-sex couples might marry for political reasons. For example,

> One problem with gay marriage is that people might marry out of duty to the community for having won the right or in some sort of protest to those who think that we shouldn't marry because we are gay. Those won't be good marriages.

GLBT people believed that same-sex marriage will have opposing effects on same-sex partnerships: to make them more serious and more fanciful. Participants also indicated that these effects on partnerships will also reflect out to affect the GLBT community.

Looking Further into Expectations of Same-sex Marriage and Partnerships

In addition to describing the dialectical tension between same-sex marriage's potential to make same-sex partnerships more serious and more fanciful, GLBT people who responded to the online survey also discussed further expectations about how they foresaw same-sex marriage affecting their own romantic relationship and same-sex romantic relationships in general. While a small portion of the sample (6%) indicated that they did not see the legal recognition of same-sex marriage as having any impact on their understanding of romantic relationships, the majority of the GLBT people in the study did see introduction of legally recognized same-sex marriage as something that would or was already influencing their experience of romantic relationships. The ways that the possibility of same-sex marriage was seen to be influential on experiences of same-sex relationships fall into two themes: same-sex marriage made relationships seem more real and same-sex marriage revealed previously unknown desires.

Making relationships seem more real. The legal recognition of same-sex marriage presents same-sex couples with the unique experience of having a new option for the performance of romantic relationships introduced after they have presumably established a system of relational expression and maintenance (Rostosky et al., 2006; Slater, 1995). The possible influence of same-sex marriage on the understanding of existing relationships is even more interesting when you recognize that same-sex couples may have developed their system of relating, in part, in reaction to the lack of institutional recognition for their relationship. GLBT people discussed how the possibility of legally recognized same-sex marriage made romantic relationships seem more real in two ways.

First, GLBT people explained how same-sex marriage would allow their relationships to be "seen" by others, including civil authorities and specific non-GLBT people in their lives. Many GLBT people saw same-sex marriage as changing the way they thought about existing romantic relationships not because of dynamics within the relationship, but because marriage had the potential to shift the way that outsiders saw the relationship. For example,

> I guess same-sex marriage does change the way I see our relationship, and other lesbian and gay relationships, too. I mean, I feel the same way about my partner—I love her no matter what—but I feel like our relationship will be just different, better, because other people will have to see our relationships as real now.

GLBT people recognized that the civil benefits of legally recognized same-sex marriage may alter the place of same-sex relationships in society. For the most part, they expressed this in terms of making relationships more real, serious, or secure. For example,

> I feel strange saying this, but being able to get a real marriage license from the state and share benefits like health insurance, property ownership, and even sharing taxes makes gay relationships seem like they really count all of a sudden. I mean, yeah, of course they counted before, but now with all the legal stuff, they just seem to count more somehow.

Another person stated,

> Having the legal protections of marriage makes me think of my 5 year relationship in a different way because the government will finally have to acknowledge it. It just seems more serious, like a new level. I want us to get married and then we can be more secure than we ever could without it.

Further, another person related her altered view of her relationship and civil recognition of same-sex marriage in patriotic terms:

> Same-sex marriage not only makes me take my relationship more seriously, it's making me take my country more seriously. I always felt oppressed and not a part of America, not really. But this seems like finally there is a light in the dark, like finally it's going to be ok to be a dyke and the government is saying that my relationship counts and I count, too. Now I just feel like I'd better not mess up my relationship up since it's so important finally.

GLBT people also discussed how they anticipated more recognition and acceptance for their same-sex relationships from non-GLBT people in their lives. Among the most commonly mentioned non-GLBT people were family members. For example,

> I think that same-sex marriage has just made me see my relationship as more important now and that has made me more bold because my expectations for us being acknowledged by my family has changed. Honestly, they have started to change already, being more open to talk about us and even inviting my partner places by name. Civil benefits are great and important, but for me, family benefits are what's really changing.

Employers were also commonly mentioned as key non-GLBT people who might see the same-sex relationship differently now that marriage was to be possible. For example,

> It is so great now that we will be able to get married. I feel like our relationship is real, important, matters more now. One thing that really made me feel this way is when my boss came to give me information about employee spousal benefits—it was right after the court decision was announced—and said that she looked forward to getting them for me. I wanted to cry.

Other GLBT people in the study discussed how marriage provides a definition of same-sex relationships that is easier for "straight" people to understand. For example,

> I am so excited about getting married—we have been together for 11 years and want to get married right away—because I will feel like I will have a real solid relationship when I can prove it to people. People like doctors and neighbors and all kinds of straight people. I won't have to explain it anymore, I will say this is my husband. Sounds great, right? Husband.

Importantly, the GLBT participants didn't just anticipate greater recognition and acceptance for their romantic relationships as a result of possible same-sex marriage, but the GLBT people themselves viewed their relationships differently because of this anticipated change in others' attitudes.

Second, GLBT people described how the possibility of same-sex marriage made them reconsider their view of their existing relationships. GLBT men and women explained that the option to legally marry makes their existing relationships seem more concrete, solid, and real to them. For example,

> I've considered myself to be in a committed relationship for a long time. But, there is something to the word marriage that makes it feel more real and serious even to me. That word, marriage, makes it mean something different because it makes it a more concrete thing to be in this relationship.

Another person stated, "Getting married and having it be legal binds us together in a more tangible way. It makes our love seem more real, even to us."

Others described how the possibility of same-sex marriage changed their view of commitment ceremonies. While Stiers (1999) describes the ways in which same-sex couples work to engender meaning in their commitment or relationship celebrating rituals without the benefit of legal recognition, participants in my study reflected the disappointment with commitment ceremonies among some members of the GLBT community. For example,

> Legal recognition makes having a ceremony seem like a real option that actually means something now, not just some sort of parody or pretend wedding. I guess that's harsh, but we talked about having a ceremony before (we've been together 8 years) and I never wanted to do it because it seemed sad to me that we could have an empty ritual that just made it seem like we were pretending it counted the same as straight weddings. But, I want to do it now because it does count and the whole thing has made me think that you can't really be totally committed without it.

Another person stated,

> I don't know, but it seems like now that we can get married legally I finally feel that I can have the kind of relationship my parents did—they were together for over 40 years because they never gave up. I know that you shouldn't have to get married to have a good relationship, but now we can start out with a real wedding, not just some made-up ritual, and it seems like that will make it easier for us work on staying committed.

Other GLBT people felt a change in their understanding of an existing relationship as a result of the impending legal recognition of same-sex marriage, but unlike the examples above, this change was towards increased instability and uncertainty. For example,

> I'm happy that we are gaining legal rights, but I've also been nervous when I think about same-sex marriage and what it means for me. My partner and I have been together for 3 years, but I'm not really sure what having the option to get married will mean for us. Would doing it really be a good thing? I guess now that marriage is a real option, I'm not so sure how real my relationship is.

Another person stated,

> Ever since we heard that same-sex marriage was going to be legal, my boyfriend and I have been fighting about this. I don't want to get married and he does. I think I am beginning to realize that I just don't want to make that kind of promise to him. This wasn't an issue before cause it couldn't really happen, but now it's a big problem.

One person's statement exemplified the tension many were feeling about the inevitability of same-sex marriage influencing same-sex relationships,

> People say that getting married doesn't change your relationship. But, I don't think that's true or why would everyone make such a big deal about getting married. I'm not sure I want my relationship to change, but just having the option to marry, whether we use it or not, is changing us already.

GLBT people explained that the impact of same-sex marriage on same-sex relationships is seen as extending beyond the legal benefits of civil recognition and affects the vision of same-sex relationships both from within and outside of same-sex couples. They understood same-sex marriage as making same-sex relationships more real to others and to the partners themselves. The ability for same-sex marriage to make same-sex relationships seem more tangible was seen as a benefit by some, but a burden by others.

Revealing desires. In addition to making same-sex partnerships seem more real, legally recognized same-sex marriage also revealed previously unknown, and often surprising, desires among the GLBT people who participated in my study. The revelation of desires as an outcome of the possibility of same-sex marriage occurred in two ways.

First, GLBT people who were not currently involved in a romantic relationship, or involved in a non-serious relationship, understood legally recognized same-sex marriage as affecting their perceptions of future relationships by revealing desired characteristics for potential partners. The legal recognition of same-sex marriage plunges GLBT adults into the unusual position of having to consider a previously unavailable relational option during their adult lives. Many participants in the study found themselves reconsidering what characteristics they seek in a potential relational partner because legally recognized marriage became available to same-sex couples. This reconsideration took many by surprise, as expressed in the following example:

> I didn't think that the court's decision about same-sex marriage would affect me too much because I'm single, but I have to admit that it has. I've found myself meeting new people and actually wondering, 'Would he be marriage material?' I guess I didn't think about the long term potential of relationships as much before.

Others registered a new level of caution about the characteristics of potential partners as a result of legally recognized same-sex marriage. For example,

Now that we can get married, I am trying to be more cautious about who I get involved with. I guess I have higher standards now. I worry I will get involved with someone who wouldn't make a good spouse down that line, and I want to avoid that if possible. It's strange, but I feel like I value the possibility of a commitment more now and am much more careful.

Same-sex marriage impacted some GLBT people's perception of future relationships by functioning as a new type of test for potential partners. For example,

I think same-sex marriage is great because it can be used as a wonderful tool to weed out the potential partners from the players. I've been on a few first dates since the court decision, and I can tell I'm checking people out in a different way now that I can bring up the marriage topic and see their reaction to it. I know I want someone who wants to build a relationship, and if they are happy about legal marriage, that's a point in their favor. If they squirm around when it comes up, I know they won't work right away.

While the previous examples were from people who were interested in marrying someday, GLBT people who were not interested in ever marrying also saw same-sex marriage as changing their view on perspective partners. For example:

I don't want to get married so [same-sex marriage] is going to make it harder for me to find a person to be in a relationship with. I know that because I don't want to get married, women will think I'm not a good potential partner, and move on. I now have to be more careful to put my feelings about marriage out there early in meeting someone so I don't get hurt later. It sucks, because before I felt like there were more potential people for me, and now I have to limit myself to the other non-marrying kinds out there. Like finding a great girl wasn't already hard enough!

The legal recognition of same-sex marriage influences not only those already involved in romantic relationships, but also those members of the GLBT community who are seeking potential partners because the possibility to marry influences their perspective on characteristics they desire in a potential partner and functions as a tool to discern whether or not a potential partner has desirable characteristics.

In addition to realizing their desires for partner characteristics, GLBT people expressed the ways in which the possibility of same-sex marriage unearthed their desire for idealized relational characteristics. Both partnered and single GLBT people expressed the way in which the legal recognition of same-sex marriage revealed their own desires for or resistance to a romantic ideal for relationships.

First, participants indicated that legally recognized same-sex marriage led them to realize their desire for idealized, "traditional," romance in their relationships. Many GLBT people who participated in the study admitted that the possibility of same-sex marriage made them realize that there were aspects of relationships associated with "fairytale" heterosexual weddings and marriages that they desired for their own relationships. For example,

> Since marriage became legal, I've realized I've been suppressing my desire for certain things in my relationship for a long time. I always thought that because I was gay, I would never have the big fancy wedding and the honeymoon and anniversary parties and the professional wedding photos framed everywhere in the house, but I now see I can have all of that, and damn it, I want it!

Another person focused on the idealized romance of a wedding itself,

> When I was growing up I was just like any little girl, I guess. I fantasized about my wedding day—the gown, flowers, limo, all that. But, when I realized I was a lesbian, I let all of that go. But, now that we can get married, I realize that I don't have to miss out on a romantic dream wedding.

The participants discussed the debate over finding the right language for same-sex relationships (Stiers, 1999) by pointing out that the word "marriage" was in itself more romantic than the terms for committed relationships used currently to refer to same-sex couples. For example,

> The legal decision is great because it puts the romance in the way we can now describe relationships. I mean, we can talk about 'getting married,' 'having a wedding,' and those words will be legally accurate. I even think the words 'husband' and 'wife' are romantic. I mean, isn't it so much more romantic that saying we are having a 'commitment ceremony' and have a 'partner?'

Some GLBT people talked of same-sex marriage in terms of revealing their desire for romance, but also revealing some problems with how such romance should be carried out in same-sex relationships. Consider the issue of applying an idealized romantic engagement script to a same-sex relationship as described by one woman:

> Having marriage be legal has made my girlfriend and I really seriously consider getting married. We've been together a while, so it would be practical and romantic. But, we now have a problem: getting engaged. Both of us want to be surprised by a romantic proposal and get a diamond ring, and of course neither of us wants to be the one asked after the other. We both want to be the 'girl' in the traditional engagement story. Obviously, we can't pull that fairytale engagement off, but we are having a hard time coming up with an equally romantic alternative.

Another person expressed frustration with adapting the romantic aspects of a traditional wedding to a same-sex ceremony,

There are many aspects of a Jewish wedding that my boyfriend and I think are really romantic and want to have in ours, but the problem is they are so gendered. We want to do this stuff, but are having a hard time figuring out how to adapt them to two men and keeping the traditional part that makes them so romantic to both of us.

In contrast to the GLBT people who expressed the ways that the possibility of legally recognized same-sex marriage revealed their desire for idealized romantic aspects of relationships, others explained how the possible legal recognition of same-sex marriage has revealed their resistance to "romance." For example,

I think it's great that we have a legal right to protect our partnerships, but I'm really disappointed that now gay people will expect to act like straight people when it comes to expressing commitment. Whenever I think of having a big wedding day I get really anxious. I didn't think I was so against the fairytale images of weddings and marriage, but I guess I am, especially for gay people. Shouldn't we be beyond it?

Others resisted the complications that come from enacting the traditional romantic wedding script. For example,

One of the great things about being a lesbian was that I would never have to be a bride in the traditional sense. Do you know how much work it is to plan a big wedding and reception? It takes away from focusing on the actual commitment you are making. I know we could just have a 'small wedding,' but then it wouldn't fit that romantic image of weddings and wouldn't be satisfying. I'd rather avoid it all together, but probably can't now that same-sex marriage is legal.

The final way in which GLBT people described same-sex marriage as revealing resistance to a romantic ideal was through rejecting an externally imposed traditional relational timeline. For example,

I think the reality of same-sex marriage is just hitting me. I guess that now LGBT people will fall into the 'first comes love, then comes marriage...' trap that our society puts out there. Now we will have to fit into that neat linear view of love and I just don't see love as that uncomplicated.

In revealing GLBT people's desires for or resistance to a romantic ideal in relationships, legally recognized same-sex marriage is influencing their implicit theories of relationships, or their belief system about relationships. This is significant because implicit theories of relationships have been shown to influence people's systems for understanding their relationships and affect their relational satisfaction, stability, and feelings towards partners (Knee, Nanayakkara, Vietor, Neighbors, & Patrick, 2001; Knee, Patrick, & Lonsbary, 2003; Sprecher & Metts, 1999). Because the GLBT people who participated in my study described how the possibility of same-sex marriage was affecting their relational perceptions, expectations, and desires, the study suggests that whether a same-sex couple marries or not, same-sex marriage may have an influence on their relational outcomes.

Introduction of Legally Recognized Same-sex Marriage as a New Context

As discussed earlier, it is a basic tenant of the study of communication in personal relationships that our communication with one another is affected by and affects the context of the interaction. Surra and Perlman (2003) point out that within communication studies, context has been conceptualized in two ways: first, as a set of structural and cultural forces external to a couple that combine to influence relationship processes, and second as something resulting from the relationship itself. Both views of context apply to same-sex marriage as a context for the understanding the relationships of GLBT people.

In 2004, the external structure of legal relationship recognition radically changed for American same-sex couples. Although various forms of domestic partnerships and civil unions had been available to same-sex couples in some U.S. locations previously (see Purcell, 1998, and Human Rights Campaign, n.d., for reviews), in 2004 Massachusetts became the first U.S. location in which same-sex couples could receive the same civil benefits as married different-sex couples. Legally recognized same-sex marriage creates a new legal, societal, and symbolic entity that same-sex relational partners may use to institutionalize their married relationships or as a counterpoint for the definition of their unmarried relationships. After Massachusetts began recognizing same-sex marriage, some states followed suit while other states introduced new laws or state constitutional amendments limiting legal marriage to that between one man and one woman. In states where same-sex marriage has been banned, same-sex couples have endured a political battle about their relationships and are faced with an external structural limit on their relationship recognition. The new relational context of same-sex marriage should be recognized as affecting same-sex couples and their social networks in states that do and those that do not legally recognize same-sex marriage.

Same-sex marriage is also a new context in the sense that it is created by the relationship between partners. Partners in all types of relationships can be understood to create a unique context for their relationship through establishing a system of rules, expectations, and behavior within the relationship (Argyle & Henderson, 1984; Baxter, Dun, & Sahlstein, 2001). This idea of creating context is particularly salient when considering same-sex newlyweds as they have the added advantage/burden of creating context in a type of relationship that is both controversial and previously unrecognized by law. Same-sex couples who have married in the first decade of legal recognition in America may be seen as creating a benchmark from which to view the new phenomenon of same-sex marriage. GLBT people also described how the new possibility of legally recognized same-sex marriage was affecting their romantic relationship and their desires regarding relationships. We might expect that as same-sex marriage continues and becomes more widely available, its existence will continue to affect the relationship experiences and expectations of GLBT people.

It is interesting to note that the GLBT people who participated in my study were those who were mostly older and in an established relationship. Further, same-sex marriage was just introduced when the study was conducted. As suggested by Marzullo and Herdt (2011), it is likely that as same-sex marriage becomes more widely available, GLBT youth will approach their relationships with the option of marrying having always been a part of their relational context. My study showed that the introduction of same-sex marriage affected GLBT people's relational desires, expectations, and perceptions. D'Augelli, Rendina, Sinclair and Grossman (2006) have found that the same-sex marriage movement has affected GLBT youth's relationship desires, expectations, and perceptions of relationships. Yet, more research will be needed to best understand the effect of same-sex marriage and the surrounding debates on GLBT youth, their identity, and their relationships. It is possible that the increasing availability and support for same-sex marriage in America may help to alleviate some the "minority stress" and its negative effects on GLBT youth (D'Augelli et al., 2006; Marzullo & Herdt, 2011). Yet, it is also possible that the fight against same-sex marriage and resulting marriage bans may have a deleterious effect on GLBT youth. It should be kept in mind that same-sex marriage is a context that affects youth as well as adults.

Same-sex marriage as a context for communication within relationships is best understood as neither an external force nor a product of the relationship, but as both simultaneously. In my study of early perceptions and understanding of legally recognized same-sex marriage, the dialectical themes discussed by participants illustrate not only the contradictory and interdependent meanings of same-sex marriage, but also that same-sex marriage is being defined by the GLBT community while simultaneously redefining the meaning of the GLBT community. This interplay is seen in the participants' understanding of same-sex marriage at the three interdependent levels of same-sex partnerships, the GLBT community, and the relationship between the GLBT community and non-GLBT community members. Many of the expectations about same-sex marriage found in my study were later echoed in research by Schulman, Gotta, and Green (2012) examining expectations about same-sex marriage in California. Further, GLBT people discussed how the possibility of same-sex marriage affected how they viewed their own relationships, how they expected others to view their relationships, and their own desires regarding relationships.

It is important to note that at the time my study was conducted, the future of same-sex marriage in Massachusetts and across the nation was uncertain. As further discussion in this book will show, as the institution of same-sex marriage spreads, matures, and is challenged, the evolving understanding of same-sex marriage and the battles surrounding it also continue to develop. As I examine experiences of same-sex marriage further, I do so from the foundation of this early study which showed that same-sex marriage should be understood as dynamic, complex, and multidimensional context for the relationships of GLBT people, same-sex couples, and their social networks.

Should We Get Hitched? Same-sex Couples Deciding to Marry or Not

I was living in Boston in 2004 when Masachusetts became the first U.S. state to have legally recognized same-sex marriage. After the initial surprise and elation of learing about this historic change in relationship recognition, my friends and I turned our thoughts to our own relationships. What were couples going to do now? Within my social circle, there were many long-term same-sex couples. Most of these couples had never given much thought to symbolically expressing their devotion to one another through something like a commitment ceremony, but many of them shared a common social network, were involved with each other's families, owned property together, had designated each other as beneficiaries in their life insurance policies or wills, had assigned each other as health care proxies or given one another durable power of attorney, had pets together, and/or were raising a child together. Although these relationships were well established, they were now considering marriage for the first time. And, despite their commitment to each other, the decision to marry or not was not an easy, no-brainer decision for most couples. Rather, these couples deliberated privately, and sometimes publicly, about the pros and cons of getting married. While some of my friends are now happily married to a same-sex partner, others remain in a committed, non-married same-sex partnership. What happened among my friends is a small glimpse into what some same-sex couples experience when legally recognized marrage becomes a possiblity for them.

This chapter examines the experiences of same-sex couples as they decide whether or not to marry. First, this chapter focuses on the attractions and obstacles to marriage faced by same-sex couples who decide to marry. Then, the chapter focuses on the experiences of same-sex couples who live in regions where they can legally marry, but decide not to do so.

Attractions and Obstacles When Considering Same-sex Marriage

When the topic of same-sex marriage comes up conversations, I'm often struck by some of the comments put forth by people who are not members of the GLBT community. I've heard "straight" people say, "Of course a gay couple would want to get married. That's the normal way of being a committed couple, right?" and, in contrast, "Why would lesbians want to get married? Don't they realize that now they can just walk away if it doesn't work out?" Inherent in these comments is an understanding of marriage as a way of institutionalizing commitment. The underlying idea is that marriage is a type of structural constraint that contributes to the stability of the couple (see Johnson, 1991; Surra, Hughes, & Jacquet, 1999). Marriage is seen to function like a civil, social, and often religious fence built around a relationship that makes it much harder to get out of the relationship and much easier to protect what you have within the relationship. But, missing from these comments is an understanding that legally recognized marriage, and the decision to get married or not, may not be the same when experienced by different-sex couples and same-sex couples.

Research has consistently shown that characteristics of commitment in committed different-sex and same-sex couples are more similar than different (see Kurdek, 2004, for overview). For example, Haas and Stafford (1998, 2005) found that same-sex couples utilized many of the same relational maintenance behaviors used by different-sex couples. Kurdek (2000) found that the process by which relationship attractions and constraints affected a partner's commitment to the relationship was similar for different-sex and same-sex couples. Gottman et al. (2003) found that the emotional qualities of same-sex couples' conflicts predicted relationship stability and satisfaction in ways similar to different-sex couples.

While there are similarities between different-sex and same-sex couples, there are also key differences that underscore the need for researchers to consider the unique experiences of same-sex couples (see Kurdek, 1991). For example, same-sex partners may not be as governed by gender norms as different-sex partners (for overviews see Patterson et al., 1999; Rutter & Schwartz, 2000). Same-sex couples are also less likely to share children or have financial arrangements similar to different-sex couples (Patterson et al., 1999). And, a significant difference between the commitment experiences in different-sex and same-sex relationships stems from the stigmatized and non-institutionalized status of same-sex relationships. The lack of normative institutional status for same-sex couples may lead to unique methods for creating and enacting commitment (DiPlacido, 1998; Patterson et al., 1999). Haas and Stafford (2005) suggest that, compared to married different-sex couples, same-sex couples without legal validation and protection for their relationships engage in maintenance behaviors meant to "check the pulse" of the relationship more often. Researchers have suggested that the lack of societal norms and constraints for same-sex relationships empowers some couples to have commitment without sexual exclusivity (LaSala, 2001; Worth, Reid, & McMillan, 2002). Because same-sex couples are often stigmatized, members of same-sex couples may be more likely to receive support and acceptance from a "chosen" family of friends rather than from their families-of-origin, and may only be fully recognized as a couple within that chosen group (Kurdek & Schmitt, 1987; Weston, 1991). Discrimination against GLBT people may lead to the couple's status being completely or partially closeted, and staying in the closet may become a relational maintenance behavior (Patterson & Schwartz, 1994). Thus, unlike most different-sex couples, some same-sex couples may actively perform their relational commitment only in select situations and contexts. How, then, does the availability of legally recognized same-sex marriage affect the commitment experience and expression for same-sex couples?

Legally recognized same-sex marriage represents a change in the stigmatized and non-institutionalized context of same-sex partnerships. For same-sex couples for whom it is available, legally recognized same-sex marriage offers a new means of expressing and enacting commitment. Still, the decision to marry may be a complicated one (see Badgett, 2009). When considering marriage, same-sex couples may consider a variety of issues in addition to their level of commitment to one another. For example, the introduction of legally recognized same-sex marriage comes when couples may have long ago established their means of expressing and enacting commitment without marriage (Rostosky, Riggle, Dudley, & Wright, 2006). Such couples may be unsure of how marriage may change the ways they experience commitment. Couples may also find themselves negotiating their expression of relational commitment within the philosophical and political battles over same-sex marriage both within and outside of the GLBT community. While same-sex marriage may be a step towards the acceptance of same-sex relationships on a societal level, it does not mean that the stigmatization of individual relationships will end.

To better understand the relationship between same-sex couple commitment and legally recognized marriage, I conducted a study of narrative descriptions of same-sex couples' discussions leading to their decision to marry (see Lannutti, 2008). I expected that factors that attracted same-sex couples to marriage would reflect the value they see in having an institutionalized relationship. Factors that deterred same-sex couples from marriage, and the ways they deal with such deterrents, would reflect the difficulties faced by same-sex couples as they attempted to express and enact their commitment in a changing relational context. The study was conducted in Massachusetts a little over a year after the state began issuing marriage licenses to same-sex couples. Two hundred sixty-three GLBT people who were either engaged to a same-sex partner (28%) or had married a same-sex partner (72%) completed an online survey about their discussions with their partners when deciding to get married or engaged.[1]

All of the GLBT people who participated in the study reported at least one attraction and one obstacle that they and their partners discussed when deciding to marry. On average, each participant reported three attractions and two obstacles to marriage. However, only 42% of the participants offered explanations of how they overcame an obstacle to marriage.

Attractions to Marriage for Same-sex Couples

Three main types of reasons to marry, or attractions to marriage, were prominent in the reported discussions that same-sex couples had when deciding to marry. These attractions centered upon the relationship between the couple and general society, the relationship between the couple and their social network, and the couple's relationship to each other.

Between the couple and general society. The first type of attraction to marriage had to do with the interaction between the same-sex couple and general society. One part of this attraction to marriage had to do with legal protections and civil benefits for the couple. GLBT people reported that they and their partner discussed getting married because "if we got married we could share insurance," "getting married makes it a lot easier to share property and money," and "we thought we should get married so that we could better take care of each other as we got older or if someone got sick...nobody could take our right to provide for each other away." These reasons match up with the expectation that same-sex marriage would allow same-sex couples to have civil and legal equality with different-sex couples discussed in Chapter 2.

Another part of the attraction to marriage related to the interaction between the couples' commitment and the general community focused on having children. Specifically, participants indicated that they believed that getting married would make it easier to bring children into their lives or protect their relationships with the children they already had. For example, "we really want to have kids someday, so we decided to get married because it would make adoptions easier." Another person stated, "We talk about having children all the time. When we could get married, we did so that it would be clear to everyone, especially the state, that the kids were ours— ours together." Another example is offered in the statement of a man talking about his partner and their adopted son,

> When we adopted our son 5 years ago, we did all this paperwork to protect our family. When it became clear that we might be able to marry, we talked about it a lot. It felt like maybe after that marriage, nobody could threaten our family.

Couples also decided to get married because of a desire to make a public statement of their commitment to one another. People who participated in the study explained that they and their partner talked about getting married in the following ways: "getting married gave us a chance to let the world know how committed we were to each other," and "for us, marriage was a way to say 'we want to be together and you can hold us to it' to everyone." Many participants indicated that they and their partner had a strong, longstanding commitment, but that legally recognized marriage was a new way of communicating that commitment to society. For example, "We've been together and committed to each other forever, but getting married was the first time we could really show that and have it known to society the way that straight people have always been able to do." For some couples who had a commitment ceremony before marriage was legally recognized, same-sex marriage was a way to publicly reaffirm their commitment. For example,

> We were married years before the state started doing it in a commitment ceremony in our church. Then, we felt like we were making a public statement of our love and commitment. Legal marriage has given us a chance to do it again.

The final part of the attractions to marriage that relate to the relationship between the committed couple and the general community includes political reasons for marriage. Responses in this category reflect participants' placement of their commitment within the public debate over GLBT rights. For example,

> We couldn't decide whether to get married or not, but we finally decided to not so much for ourselves, but for all of those lesbian and gay couples who can't get married yet. It seemed wrong to be a committed couple with the right, and not to use it.

Another person stated, "Getting married was important for us so that we could stand up and be counted. We want our presence felt when they try to take marriage away from us in the future."

Between the couple and their social network. The second type of reason for getting married discussed by same-sex couples had to do with the relationship between the couple and their friends and family, or social network. Some couples thought that same-sex marriage would lead to an increase in acknowledgment from friends or family members. They reported that getting married would give family and friends an opportunity to share in and cele-brate their relationship. For example, "We've been to so many weddings for our straight friends and we thought it was time for them to celebrate our relationship in the same way," and "Our families have been really supportive of our relationship and they wanted a big party for us, which is really nice."

GLBT people also thought that getting married would define their rela-tionship in the same terms that their heterosexual friends and family used to define their seriously committed relationships, and that this would help their social networks recognize the nature of their relationships. As one woman stated, "My folks like my partner, but would call her my 'friend.' We wanted them to see her as my wife, just like they see my brother's wife." Another man explained, "Our straight friends all had husbands and wives, but they saw us as 'boyfriends.' One reason we got married was so it would sink in that we were 'husbands,' too."

Participants saw marriage as a means of solidifying their relationship's place within their families especially. For example, "being married means he is part of my family" and "even though my family was accepting, getting married really made us a lifelong couple in my family's eyes…she is one of us now." The topic of same-sex marriage and families-of-origin is a complex one that will also be discussed as an obstacle to getting married in this chapter and will be further explored in Chapter 4.

Between the members of the couple. The final type of attraction to marriage that emerged from the descriptions of the same-sex couples' discussions about whether to marry focuses on partners and their relationship with one an-other. As you might expect, couples' feelings for each other were a reason to marry. Participants said, "we wanted to get married because we are in love," "we want to spend our lives together," and "getting married showed each other how deeply we feel." GLBT people also mentioned religious reasons for marriage. For example, one person explained that he and his partner "felt that you can't have commitment without God, so that was part of why we got married." Another said, "we wanted to bless our union."

GLBT people described three types of attractions to marriage discussed between them and their partners when deciding to marry. Some of these reasons to marry centered upon the interchange between the couple and the general society, including their desire for legal protection and civil benefits for their relationship, their belief that marriage would help them protect or have children, their desire to make a public statement of their commitment to one another, and political motivations for marriage. Other reasons to marry had to do with the relationship between the couple and their social network. Same-sex couples discussed how marriage would lead to greater acknowledgement of their relationship and a clearer definition of their relationship in the minds of family and friends. Finally, same-sex couples wanted to get married for reasons related to their relationship to each other, including their feelings for one another and their religious beliefs. Many of these reasons to marry have been echoed in other research on same-sex marriage. Badgett (2009) studied same-sex marriage in the Netherlands and found that some Dutch couples mentioned a "practical spark" that lead them to marry, such as the desire for children. Badgett (2009) also found that Dutch same-sex couples saw legal benefits, the opportunity to express their commitment to each other, the opportunity to make a political statement, and the opportunity to express their commitment to family and friends as benefits of marriage. As will be discussed in Chapter 5, older same-sex couples in the U.S. also see same-sex marriage as a means of gaining financial, medical, and relational security and social network and political recognition for same-sex couples.

Obstacles to Marriage for Same-sex Couples

As mentioned above, all of the GLBT people who participated in the study also discussed at least one obstacle to getting married that they and their partners considered when deciding to get married. As with attractions to marriage, there were three types of obstacles to marriage discussed by the same-sex couples. The first two types of obstacles to marriage mirror the types of attractions to marriage in that the first type of obstacle related to the interchange between the couples and general society, and the second type of obstacle related to the relationship between the couples and their social network. The third type of obstacle to marriage focused on practical and symbolic problems with weddings and the institution of marriage.

Between the couple and general society. The first type of obstacle to getting married discussed by the same-sex couples had to do with the interaction between the couple and society in general. These obstacles related to the civil and legal limitations of same-sex marriage in Massachusetts at the time the data was collected. At the time of data collection, Massachusetts was the only U.S. state granting equal marriage rights to same-sex couples and different-sex couples. At this time, the same-sex marriages in Massachusetts were available only to residents, did not have federal recognition, and were not transferable to other states. These limitations concerned participants. For example,

> One thing that made us wait to get married was the fact that to really stay married we would have to stay in MA. We felt like we weren't just committing to each other, but the state as well. The state was actually the tough commitment to make.

Another participant stated, "We almost didn't get married because it has no federal recognition. So, in legal terms, we are half married I guess." Another participant joked about the limited scope of same-sex marriage,

> We thought about not getting married until it was legal in the whole U.S., but we probably won't live to be 300. So, now when people ask if we're married, we say 'yeah, but not when we're away on vacation.'

The couples' concerns about the civil and legal limitations of marriage are similar to those found by Porche, Purvin, and Waddell (2005). Although same-sex marriage has become more widely available in the United States and has gained federal recognition since these couples were considering marriage, same-sex marriage is still available in a fraction of the states. Thus, concerns about the limitations of legal recognition for same-sex marriage are still relevant.

Other participants indicated that unresolved previous marriages served as barriers to marrying their current partner. For example,

> I was married to a woman, and we never bothered with a divorce after we split up since it was clear that I would never marry again. Dale and I had to wait to get married until I got a divorce from my ex-wife.

Other participants were barred from marriage until they resolved legal issues with previous same-sex partners. For example, "We both still had shared property with exes we needed to work out. Plus, I had a civil union in Vermont with my ex and we had to resolve that before I could get married in MA." These obstacles, although related to a previous relationship, were particularly problematic for couples because of the civil and legal limitations of same-sex marriage in the United States. Many people who had ended different-sex marriages might have resolved those marriages differently if the possibility of legally recognized same-sex marriage seemed likely at the time. Discrepancies and similarities between civil unions and marriages are often difficult to negotiate and leave couples in a state of legal uncertainty. The newness of and uncertainty surrounding legally recognized same-sex marriage formed a challenge for many same-sex couples as they considered marriage.

Between the couple and their social network. The second type of obstacle to marriage discussed by same-sex couples included problems between the couples and their social network members. Some participants mentioned challenges to their marriage presented by friends. For example, "we were upset because our friends didn't take our getting married as seriously as they took it when straight friends get married," and "we went back and forth on whether to have a wedding when some close friends said that they didn't want their kids at a gay wedding."

Although difficulties with friends were mentioned, families proved to be a greater challenge to participants. Forty-one percent of the participants indicated that family disapproval, usually parental disapproval, was an obstacle to same-sex marriage. For example, "the biggest problem for us was that our parents were totally against us getting married," "we had to deal with the fact that our families wouldn't attend our wedding or even admit we were married," and "we almost didn't get married because my parents were so angry and mean about it." One woman offered more detail about the family challenge to marriage, "It was really hard to decide to get married. Marriages are supposed be about joining families, not just a couple. But, her family is so against our relationship, we couldn't have that." A male participant offered, "We almost changed our minds about getting married. We thought our families were ok with us as a couple, but when we wanted to send out wedding invitations, his parents freaked out."

Previous studies have shown that a lack of family support has a negative impact on the quality of same-sex relationships (Caron & Ulin, 1997; Rostosky et al., 2004; Smith & Brown, 1997). Interestingly, couples were often surprised by a lack of approval for their marriage from a family member they previously perceived as supportive of their relationship. A couple choosing to express their commitment through marriage may trigger homophobic reactions previously dormant or hidden. Even though recognition of marriage from friends and family members was expressed as an attraction to marriage earlier, this need for an increase in recognition underscores the challenges presented to couples from a lack of acceptance and approval from social network members.

Previous research has also identified family disapproval, especially from parents, as a challenge faced by same-sex couples wishing to marry. For example, Badgett (2009) describes family disapproval, especially from mothers, as a barrier to marriage for same-sex couples. Yet, other research has shown that family members are often supporters of same-sex couples' marriages (Ramos, Goldberg & Badgett, 2009). Same-sex marriage experiences of same-sex couples and their families-of-origin will be discussed in more detail in Chapter 4.

Problems with weddings and marriage. The third type of obstacle that was discussed by same-sex couples considering marriage represented participants' practical and symbolic difficulties with wedding ceremonies and the institution of marriage itself. First, couples faced difficulties with funding and planning their wedding celebrations. Participants mentioned that one obstacle to getting married was paying for the wedding and reception. For example, "it was hard to come up with the money for the reception," and "we wanted to have a great celebration, but we weren't ready for how much it was going to cost."

Money was not the only obstacle to planning a wedding and reception. Participants expressed difficulties with decisions about the ceremonies themselves. For example,

> We knew right away we wanted to get married, but we almost scrapped it when we got down to discussing how we would get married. Should we do it in a church? Should we have attendants? It took forever to decide all that.

Another person explained:

> Jodie and I decided to get married, then it got hard. We didn't know where to start. Should we ask someone to give us away, or was that silly since we'd been together for years? And, the biggest problem was dealing with what to wear. She wanted us to wear traditional gowns, and I thought it would look like silly if we both did that, but I didn't want to wear a suit, either. That was hard to resolve because we didn't want our wedding to look like a drag show.

Other couples experienced difficulties in planning stemming from engagement. For example, "First, getting engaged was hard. We didn't know who should ask who? Then, should there be a ring, two rings? Then, the wedding was hard to plan, too." Another participant explained,

> Getting engaged was kind of confusing. I asked her with no ring. Then, a few days later, she got me a nice ring and asked me. So, I went and got her a ring. Then, we couldn't decide how big we wanted the wedding to be, or how traditional.

Previous research has examined the symbolic and religious meanings within the performance of gay and lesbian relationship rituals, such as holy unions and commitment ceremonies (Halderman, 1998; McQueeney, 2003; Stiers, 1999). In her study of commitment ceremonies, Stiers (1999) describes same-sex couples' struggles with creating a ceremony symbolizing commitment without gendered pitfalls or a traditional blueprint. Many of the difficulties described by Stiers (1999) are similar to those discussed by the same-sex couples in my study.

In addition to difficulties with the mechanics of getting engaged and having a wedding, same-sex couples considering marriage also discussed another obstacle to marriage: their own philosophical and political issues with the institution of marriage. For example, "we weren't sure if getting married meant that we were somehow accepting the idea that governments control relationships," and "as a feminist, I've always seen marriage as a bad deal for women...I wasn't sure if it made marriage ok just because we were both women." Similar to GLBT people's responses to same-sex marriage discussed in Chapter 2, participants in this study also expressed their concern that marriage was part of a mainstreaming of GLBT life. For example, "We kind of had a problem with a traditional wedding, and the idea of marriage altogether, because we didn't want it to seem like we were trying to be 'normal.'" Others expressed concern that getting married would make it appear that they were trying to be like heterosexual couples. For example, "When we talked about getting married, we didn't just talk about us, but whether or not marriage was a straight idea" and "I was worried that if we got married, it would seem like we needed a 'straight' label to justify our relationship." Another person explained, "We wanted to make sure our wedding wasn't like straight weddings, because our relationship certainly isn't like a straight relationship." When discussing and deciding about same-sex marriage, couples experienced the personal as political, and the political as personal. This highlights the need to consider same-sex commitment within an evolving social and political context for relationships.

Overcoming Obstacles to Same-sex Marriage

As mentioned earlier, although all of the people who participated in this study were married or engaged to a same-sex partner, they all mentioned at least one obstacle to marriage that they and their partners discussed and considered. I was interested in how the couples managed to overcome the obstacles to marriage that they faced. Interestingly, only forty-two percent of the participants in the study shared information about overcoming obstacles to marriage in their responses to my survey. The relatively low number of participants that included descriptions of how they overcame obstacles may be because the instructions, which asked them to focus on things they and their partner discussed when deciding to marry, steered participants away from solutions to obstacles. Alternately, the lack of explanations for how participants overcame obstacles may suggest that they did not fully alleviate the challenges to same-sex marriage or addressing these challenges may have been an ongoing process at the time of data collection. Of course, there is also the possibility that the obstacles remained obstacles but that the couple just learned to live with them and carried on with their marriage plans. Still, the information that was offered about how the couples dealt with the obstacles to marriage is interesting and shed light on the direct and indirect communicative strategies that couples employed as they moved toward marriage.

Direct solutions. Participants reported two ways in which they and their partners directly confronted the obstacles to same-sex marriage. First, they directly communicated with social network members who were viewed as obstacles to marriage about the issue. For example, "we had to have my parents over to dinner and talk with them about how their objections to our marriage were hurting us," "I ended up telling my so-called friends off for not being as excited about my wedding as I was about theirs," and "we each sent our parents letters explaining how much we were in love and why we were making this commitment with or without their support."

Second, couples engaged in political actions to help overcome some of the legal limitations of same-sex marriage. For example, "we decided the best way to make our marriage count everywhere is to fight...we demonstrate, we volunteer, and we give money," and "we asked all of our wedding guests to give money to [a local same-sex marriage advocacy group] and call their legislators as their gift to us." Others saw their marriage itself as part of a political solution to the limitations of same-sex marriage. For example, "We weren't going to get married because it only counts [in Massachusetts], but then we realized that's why we should get married. It was the most subversive thing we could do." Another participant explained, "the more of us that get married, the less likely it is that they can take it away, and the less likely that they can keep it away from others in other places."

Indirect solutions. Couples also dealt with obstacles to same-sex marriage in indirect ways. The most common way of overcoming the obstacles to same-sex marriage was to ignore the obstacle. For example, "we just decided not to hear people's objections and get married anyway," "we really wanted to get married, so we did and just ignored the mounting bills," and "we just ignored the people who didn't support us and didn't invite them." Although 58% of the participants who discussed ways in which they and their partners overcame obstacles to same-sex marriage indicated that they chose to ignore the obstacle, it is unclear if this is a temporary fix to a problem that may later require more direct communicative strategies to fully overcome.

Second, couples discussed the obstacle among themselves, but did not directly address the issue with the person who was creating the perceived obstacle. For example, "I was hurt because my father was horrible about us getting married, but my partner and I talked a lot and he helped me get over it." Another person explained,

> I was upset because my co-workers didn't throw me a bridal shower even though they did for every straight girl who got married. After talking to my partner, I decided not to mention it to them but just start looking for a new job.

Badgett (2009) discussed the processes used by same-sex couples to overcome barriers to marriage. Many of Badgett's (2009) processes, such as meeting family disapproval with persuasive attempts, are also reflected in the direct and indirect strategies reported by the married and engaged people in my study. Badgett (2009), however, also identified additional processes internal to the couple such as reframing the meaning of marriage to overcome issues with the institution and negotiation between partners to address disagreements about marriage. It is important to note that both my study and Badgett's (2009) were studies of couples who had decided to marry, and therefore do not reflect the experiences of unmarried same-sex couples who may have identified and discussed obstacles to marriage that they did not overcome. It is important to learn more about the experiences of same-sex couples who live in states in which they can legally marry, but choose not to do so.

Same-sex Couples Who Choose to Not Marry

Of course, not all same-sex couples who live in states where same-sex marriage is recognized choose to marry. Yet, discussed in Chapter 2, same-sex marriage has been shown to affect the way that GLBT people perceive their current romantic relationships, how GLBT people think that others perceive their relationships, and GLBT people's desires regarding relationships. Thus, legally recognized same-sex marriage can be understood as a new relational context for same-sex couples whether they marry or not. The same-sex marriage research literature, however, has mostly focused on the experiences of same-sex couples who marry. Therefore, I conducted a study to better understand the decision-making process and perspectives of same-sex couples who could legally marry in their state, but have decided against it, at least for the present time. Thirty-seven same-sex couples who lived in Massachusetts (after same-sex marriage was recognized there starting in 2004) who had been together for at least 3 years (average relationship length for the couples was 8.14 years)[2] but were not married or engaged were interviewed.[3] Concerning their intentions to remain unmarried, two types of couples emerged in the study. The first type of couple (23 couples) indicated that they had decided to never marry. The remaining couples (14 couples) decided not to marry in the near future, but indicated that they might be willing to reconsider marriage at a later time. I discussed why the couples had decided not to marry with them, and couples of both types shared six reasons to not marry. The couples who decided not to marry now, but might be willing to reconsider later, described an additional three considerations that they had discussed with one another when deciding about marriage.

Same-sex Couples' Reasons to Not Marry

The same-sex couples who could marry, but decided not to, offered six reasons why they choose to remain unmarried. First, same-sex couples decided not to marry because of resistance and/or rejection from members of their families-of-origin. Couples discussed ways in which members of their families were either not supportive of them as a couple, not supportive of the idea of marrying, or both. For example, "Our parents factored into our decision. My parents are really religious and not happy we are a couple. His parents are ok with us as a couple, but keep making negative comments about gay marriage around us." Another woman described family resistance in this way, "We know our parents won't attend our wedding if we have one. They probably wouldn't acknowledge our marriage. That would just make us sad, so we decided not to put ourselves through it."

As discussed earlier in this chapter, same-sex couples who decided to marry cited family-of-origin disapproval as the most common obstacle to marriage. Other research has also found that family members' disapproval, rejection, and resistance often provides a significant challenge to same-sex couples considering marriage (Badgett, 2009; Smart, 2007). Yet, Schechter, Tracy, Page, and Luong (2008) describe how getting married made some same-sex couples feel closer to their families and caused previously rejecting or resistant family members "mellow" to the idea of same-sex marriage. The interaction between couples and their family members in the context of same-sex marriage is complex, and serves as the focus on Chapter 4.

Another reason to not marry described by same-sex couples centered on the political implications of same-sex marriage. Some couples cited political misgivings with the institution of marriage, while others sought to avoid the "mainstreaming" effect that marriage may have on their own and other same-sex relationships. These political objections to marriage echo responses from GLBT people concerned about marriage's potentially negative effect on the GLBT community as described in Chapter 2 and some of the problems with marriage that served as obstacles to marriage for married or engaged couples discussed earlier in this chapter. Other couples decided not to marry because they objected to the focus on marriage as a means to overall equality for GLBT people in the United States. For example, "Marriage is being blown out of proportion...like if we can marry all of the discrimination against gay people will vanish. We decided to opt out of all that." The political objections to marriage discussed by the couples mirror arguments made by some GLBT activists (see Wharton & Philips, 2004).

A third reason to not marry discussed by the couples had to do with issues of "outness" and same-sex marriage. Many couples chose not to marry so that one or both partners could either remain closeted to a key audience, such as an employer, or could have more control over his or her level of "outness" than they believed to be possible once married. For example, "I'm in the Army, so it's not possible for me to marry her right now" and "My job is at a Catholic agency. They know I'm gay in my office, but if we go and get married then I guess anyone in the agency could know and that could lead to trouble." Concerns about potential dangers from the increased "outness" that is perceived to come with marriage was also a concern for older same-sex couples who are discussed in Chapter 5. Rolfe and Peel (2011) studied same-sex couples in the United Kingdom who chose not to have a civil union and also found that concerns about "outness" influenced the couples' decision to avoid a civil union. It should be noted that my interviews with the couples who choose not to marry took place after the repeal of the military's "Don't ask, don't tell" (DADT) policy in 2010, but before all branches of the U.S. military had implemented new policies as a result of the appeal of DADT. Further, the Federal Defense of Marriage Act (DOMA) had not yet been struck down by the Supreme Court at the time of the interviews. Therefore, GLBT military personnel were still experiencing uncertainty about their status and levels of "outness" at the time this data was collected. Along with employees of some religious organizations and other more conservative groups, military personnel are likely to still feel uncertainty about their ability to be fully disclosive about their sexuality and relationships. This serves as an important reminder that experiences of same-sex marriage are influenced by complex and interwoven dimensions of context.

Same-sex couples also discussed financial reasons for their decision to not marry. Some couples indicated that getting married might have a negative financial outcome for them. For example, "He has a much lower credit score than I do. Right now, we can just apply for things in my name, but if we get married, then his score will come into play." Other couples pointed to the finances associated with a wedding as a reason to not marry. As one woman stated, "We think it is foolish how much money people spend on weddings. But, we would want a nice wedding if we had one. So, we decided to avoid the whole thing." As discussed earlier in this chapter, concern about the cost of weddings was also mentioned by married or engaged same-sex couples as an obstacle to marriage.

Many same-sex couples who choose not to marry indicated that they made this choice because they did not need marriage. Some couples discussed legal arrangements that they had already made that would be redundant to the legal protections provided by marriage. For example, "We took care of legal stuff years ago. We have it all worked out for the house, retirement funding, living wills, all that. So, marriage wouldn't do us any good now." Riggle, Rostosky, and Prather (2006) found that same-sex couples who were older, more committed to each other, and more disclosive about their relationship to relatives were more likely to have engaged in this type of legal advanced planning. Somewhat ironically, combining Riggle, Rostosky, and Prather's (2006) findings and the information offered by non-married couples in this study suggests that couples who were committed enough to each other before marriage was available to seek legal protections may find those same legal protections to be a barrier to marriage after same-sex marriage became available to them.

Other couples indicate that they did not need marriage for more interpersonal reasons. Couples indicated that they already felt committed to their partner and relationship, and therefore they did not feel the need to marry. For example, "I'm glad that there is marriage now, but we've really been like married for years. No need for a piece of paper now." Concern that marriage was "just a piece of paper" is also discussed by Purvin, Porche, and Waddell (2005) in their study of same-sex couples considering marriage. Other couples indicated that they never thought of marriage as part of the relational trajectory for same-sex relationships previously and therefore did not want to marry now. One woman provided an example, "After I knew I was a lesbian, I never really thought about marrying someone. It seems like it would be weird to do that now." The idea that marriage was not considered part of a same-sex relationship trajectory, and therefore seems unnecessary now to some couples, is consistent with Recheck, Elliott, and Umberson's (2009) study of long-term same-sex couples. As discussed in Chapter 2, legally recognized same-sex marriage represents a new relational context for couples, and it should be expected that some couples, especially those who have been in committed relationships without marriage for years, would choose not to disrupt their established methods of expressing and maintaining their union by marrying.

The final reason to not marry discussed by same-sex couples had to do with limitations and uncertainty of legally recognized same-sex marriage itself. At the time of the data collection, only Massachusetts recognized same-sex marriage. The Supreme Court had not yet struck down DOMA, so the U.S. federal government was not recognizing same-sex marriages. Meanwhile, twelve states had recently enacted some sort of same-sex marriage ban which not only prevented those states from issuing marriage licenses to same-sex couples, but also prohibited them from recognizing same-sex marriages performed in other states. For these reasons, many same-sex couples choose not to marry. For example, "We have marriage here and now, but maybe only here and now. So, we thought why do it?" The limitations associated with same-sex marriage were also cited by married or engaged same-sex couples as obstacles to marriage earlier in this chapter. Although marriage recognition may have expanded since the time these interviews were conducted, same-sex marriages in the U.S. are still not available nationwide. Thus, the legal limitations of marriage can be expected to remain a barrier to marriage for many same-sex couples.

"Not now, maybe later" Couples' Same-sex Marriage Considerations

As explained above, there were two types of same-sex couples who had decided to not marry interviewed for the study: those who have decided to never marry, and those who have decided not to marry in the near future but might reconsider marriage in the future. While both types of couples shared in the six reasons to not marry discussed above, three additional considerations emerged from the interviews with the "not now, maybe later" couples.

Many of the "not now, maybe later" couples indicated that they had decided to remain unmarried for the time being because they felt that their relationship was not a point where marriage would be the right choice. Some of these couples indicated that they were simply "not ready" to marry. For example, "Marriage should be forever. We're good and have been together over 4 years, but we're not sure we are quite ready to say 'forever' yet." Other couples were experiencing relationship difficulties that contributed to their decision to not marry. For example, "We are working on some things right now...about our careers and whether we want kids. That has to be worked out before we could talk about marriage ever again."

In addition to feeling that they were not at a point in their relationship to marry, "not now, maybe later" same-sex couples discussed two considerations that explain why they might consider marriage in the future even though they have chosen to not marry in the near future. First, some couples indicated that they might consider marriage in the future if they felt that they needed the legal protections for them and their relationship that marriage could provide. For example, "I guess we would think about marriage again if we felt like we needed to protect our assets together, like a business or something." Second, some couples indicated that they might reconsider their decision to not marry if they thought that marriage might make having a family easier and more secure. As one woman stated, "We aren't sure about kids in the future. But if we do want them, we might have to think about marriage again. It could make adopting easier." Another example was provided by another couple, "If we have kids we might get married. We would want to make sure we were seen as a family legally to make it easier."

Same-sex Couples and Decisions about Marriage

When I have presented my research about same-sex couples and their decision making about whether to marry or not, I have heard from heterosexual people who say that many of the attractions and obstacles to marriage and the reasons to not marry described by the same-sex couples are similar to those considered by different-sex couples deliberating about marriage. Studies of different-sex couples offer some support to this observation.

Many studies of different-sex couples examine a couple's transition to marriage from a cost/benefit perspective (e.g., McGinnis, 2003; Oppenheimer, 2000; South, 1992). The attractions and obstacles to marriage discussed by the same-sex couples in my study could be understood as costs and benefits of marriage, although I did not compare or ask couples to compare the relative value of these costs and benefits in my study. McGinnis (2003) explains that potential costs and benefits of marriage for different-sex couples may include changes to one's financial situation and changes to one's relationships with family and friends. Such considerations were mentioned as both attractions to marriage and obstacles to marriage by same-sex couples who chose to marry and as reasons not to marry by same-sex couples who chose to not marry. Although South (1992) points out that context is an important part of understanding different-sex couples' cost-benefit attitudes about marriage, the context experienced by different-sex couples considering marriage is markedly different than the context experienced by same-sex couples considering marriage. While different-sex and same-sex couples deciding to marry or not may share some considerations, such as financial changes and changes to relationships with their social networks, same-sex couples do so in a context in which legal recognition for their marriage is relatively new and dynamic. While every couple's decision about marriage is personally life-changing, same-sex couples make these decisions in context of widespread social change and challenge. While there is value in comparing the experiences of same-sex and different-sex couples, it is important to note that the differences in context for same-sex and different-sex couples could make the experience of even a seemingly similar consideration quite different.

The studies discussed in this chapter reveal interesting similarities between same-sex couples who decided to marry and same-sex couples who decided to not marry. Both types of couples shared several considerations as they deliberated about whether to marry or not. For some shared considerations, the two types of couples seemed to have differing approaches. Some same-sex couples who choose to marry did so in order to take advantage of the legal, civil, and financial structure that comes with marriage, while some same-sex couples who choose to not marry did so in part to avoid the legal, civil, and financial structure inherent in marriage. Other considerations were viewed as problematic by the two types of couples, but the couples who choose to marry found a way to ignore or overcome the obstacle represented by the consideration. Specifically, the limitations of legally recognized same-sex marriage, financial costs associated with a wedding, and the philosophical/political issues with marriage were concerns discussed by couples who decided to marry and those that did not. Both types of couples also identified objection and/or rejection from some of their social network members as a barrier to marriage. For both types of couples, objections and/or rejection from family members was particularly problematic. Same-sex couples, marriage, and families will be explored further in Chapter 4. The similarities among the considerations discussed by same-sex couples who chose to marry and those who chose to not marry provide a more detailed picture of the decision making of same-sex couples, but also raise a number of questions. More research is needed to better understand how couples who decide to marry overcome the obstacles they face. Further research is also needed to better understand what other factors distinguish couples who face the same obstacles, but make different choices about whether to marry or not.

CHAPTER FOUR

Same-sex Marriage, Couples, and Families

A s I have surveyed and interviewed GLBT people and same-sex couples about same-sex marriage over the past decade, one important aspect of their lives seems to always enter the picture: family. As discussed in Chapter 2, GLBT people perceive same-sex marriage as a means to better protect their family unit and to gain greater relationship recognition from their family-of-orign. In Chapter 3, married and engaged same-sex couples mentioned greater protection for their family unit and greater recognition for their relationship from their family-of-origin as attractions to marriage. Yet, 41% of the married or engaged same-sex couples discussed in Chapter 3 also listed objections from family-of-origin members as an obstacle to getting married. Same-sex couples who have chosen to not marry, as discussed in Chapter 3, also listed objections or resistence from family-of-origin members as a reason to not marry. Further, some same-sex couples who do not want to marry now listed the ability to make having and protecting a family easier as a reason to possibly consider marriage in the future. Thus, I have consistently found that same-sex marriage and family, either a family unit created by the couple or families-of-origin, are intertwined.

While many studies have examined a variety of characteristics and experiences of same-sex couples and their families (see Goldberg, 2010), relatively few studies have focused specifically on same-sex marriage and families. Even fewer studies have examined same-sex marriage and families from a Communication Studies perspective. Research examining the experiences of same-sex couples and their family members when a same-sex marriage restriction is introduced in their region will be discussed in Chapter 6. The current chapter focuses on two aspects of the interchange between same-sex marriage, couples, and their families. First, I discuss a study examining the ways that same-sex couples and their family-of-origin members communicate about the couples' same-sex marriage. Then, I focus on same-sex marriage and the families created by same-sex couples.

Couples' Communication with Family-of-Origin
Members about Same-sex Marriage

When I conducted my study of the attractions and obstacles to same-sex marriage that factored into same-sex couples' decisions to marry (discussed in Chapter 3), I was struck by the fact that 41% of the participants indicated that family disapproval, and usually parental disapproval, was an obstacle to marriage for them and their partners. Yet, this previous study shed little detail on how these married and engaged same-sex couples overcame the obstacle of family disapproval because so few participants discussed strategies for overcoming obstacles, and the most popular strategy that was discussed was to ignore the obstacle. Other research presented a mixed view of family-of-origin reactions to same-sex marriage. Ramos, Goldberg and Badgett (2009) reported that 89% of their sample of married same-sex partners in Massachusetts indicated that most or all of their family members supported their marriage. Further, additional research echoed my finding that family-of-origin disapproval of their marriage is often a problem for same-sex couples (Lannutti, 2007b; Macintosh, Reissuing, & Andruff, 2010). Therefore, I wanted to learn much more about how same-sex couples were communicating with their family-of-origin members about same-sex marriage. I conducted interviews with 48 same-sex couples[1] who were either married or engaged to be married in Massachusetts about their interactions with their family-of-origin members about their decision to marry and marriage (for more details about the study, see Lannutti, 2013).[2] Although Weston (1991) argues that familial homophobia may lead GLBT people to form "families of choice" often consisting of networks of close friends, participants in this study were asked to think of those with whom they shared kinship relationships (such as adoption, biological, or marriage-based relationships) as their "family" to discuss in the interviews.

As a Communication Studies scholar, I find many aspects of family interaction to be of interest. But, for my study of the interactions about same-sex marriage between same-sex couples and their family-of-origin members, I chose to focus on one important aspect of communication: privacy regulation. Because same-sex marriage presents couples with a new means of communicating their relationship status, expressing their commitment to one another, and presenting and linking their relationship to their family, same-sex marriage may be associated with challenges to the regulation of private information among couples and their families. To help me better understand the interactions among couples and their family members, I relied on Petronio's (2002) Communication Privacy Management theory (CPM). CPM offers a means to understanding the complex process of privacy regulation in personal relationships and has been used to explain privacy management within families (e.g., Caughlin & Petronio, 2004; Petronio,

Jones, & Morr, 2003). CPM assumes a dialectical tension between privacy and disclosure. CPM posits that people feel they own private information and mark boundaries between private information held singularly or in co-ownership with others, that privacy boundaries are managed through a rule-based system, and that shared privacy boundaries must be managed through coordination with others (Petronio, 2002). Privacy rule management involves three related processes. First, there is "privacy rule foundations" which focus on privacy rule development, privacy rule attributes, and privacy rule change. Second, "privacy boundary rule coordination" focuses on the ways people manage their personal privacy boundaries and collective privacy boundaries. In other words, privacy boundary rule coordination involves managing what is private information that you control access to and how you manage the revealing and concealing of information that is private but is shared between you and others. Third, "privacy turbulence" erupts due to the complexity of managing privacy boundaries on multiple levels and in coordination with others (Petronio, 2002). CPM is predictive of smooth privacy management and situations when breakdowns in privacy regulation occur.

I found that the introduction of same-sex marriage into a family triggered changes in privacy regulation not encountered before the legal recognition of same-sex marriage. Same-sex couples' descriptions of their interactions with family members about their marriage illustrated privacy management processes described in CPM (Petronio, 2002). Three themes emerged from same-sex couples' descriptions of their interactions with family members about same-sex marriage. The first theme to emerge describes the way that legally recognized same-sex marriage served as a contextual criterion to influence privacy rule change among family members. The second theme to emerge described the ways couples and their family members negotiated sharing news of the couples' same-sex marriage. The third theme to emerge described couples' negotiation of revealing and concealing of details of their relationship with family members within the context of same-sex marriage.

Same-sex Marriage as a Context for Privacy Rule Change

According to CPM, communication privacy management is rule-governed. Therefore, it is important to understand the process by which people establish privacy rules and how and why such rules may change. Petronio (2002, 2010) describes the ways in which privacy rule foundations are developed in families and implicitly and explicitly communicated to family members. Petronio (2002) suggests people rely on five criteria (culture, gender, motivation, context, and risk-benefit ratio) at any point when privacy rules are established or changed, but that "criteria alternatively or in conjunction take the foreground…as others remain in the background" (p. 39). The importance of context as a criterion for privacy rule change was evident in same-sex couples' discussions of their interactions with family members surrounding their marriage.

As explained by Petronio (2002; 2010) and further demonstrated by Child, Petronio, Agyeman-Budu, and Westermann (2011), changes to privacy rules may be triggered by a novel or new context. Consistent with Lannutti (2005) and Chapter 1, many participants in this study discussed same-sex marriage and/or their own decision to marry as forming a "new situation," "new area," or "new playing field" for them and their families. Thus, legally recognized same-sex marriage served as a new relational context for same-sex couples and their family members. Married or engaged couples were not only redefining their relationship via same-sex marriage, but the couples expected their family members to accept their new relationship definition. For many families, this new definition of the couple served as a catalyst for privacy rule changes that took various forms.

For many couples, the privacy rule changes between them and their families brought about by same-sex marriage was immediately evident. For example,

> Elvis: I knew that the minute we decided to get married that certain things about how we talked to our families, well, my family really, would have to change.
> Researcher: What things would change exactly?
> Elvis: I guess that we would have to be more direct with them…tell them more about us and our plans than before.

Other couples described same-sex marriage as a criterion for changing privacy rules among family members, but in a less sudden way than previously described. For example,

> Georgia: After we got married, I noticed the way that some people talked about us changed.
> Researcher: Can you give me some examples of what you are talking about?
> Georgia: Well, I started to notice little things after a while. I just noticed that my sister would tell her friends more about us…what we were doing, us buying a house…than she did before.

These examples illustrate that same-sex marriage and/or couples' decisions to marry functioned as a contextual criteria that could affect privacy rule change for both internal (e.g., how Elvis and his partner would talk to family members about their relationship) and external (e.g., Georgia's sister discussing Georgia and her partner with her sister's friends) family privacy boundaries. The examples provided by Elvis and Georgia highlight the way that same-sex marriage was a catalyst for more permeable internal and external family privacy boundaries, but later examples will show how despite the legal recognition associated with same-sex marriage, couples were not always treated according to the typical internal family privacy rules for some families. Georgia's example also highlights the way that privacy rule change was often implicitly accepted by couples and their families. For other families, changes to privacy rules were explicitly discussed and sometimes rejected. For example,

> Amanda: I was at my mom's house and I heard her on the phone with one of her friends. She was clearly giving an update on her kids, but when she talked about me she didn't even mention Maddie. Just my job. When she got off I asked her why she didn't mention Maddie or anything about my relationship. She just shrugged.
> Maddie: Yeah. But there was more to it you told me.
> Amanda: I told her we were married now and it hurts me that she still talks about us differently than my sister and her husband. She wouldn't talk much about it. I know she still does it, though.

Changes to privacy rules among family members triggered by same-sex marriage were often challenging for both the couples and their family members. Some couples were uncomfortable with the changes leading to what they perceived as less privacy for them. Other couples expressed negative outcomes, such as hurtful emotions, when family members rejected what couples perceived to be changed privacy rules. These experiences highlight the importance of recognizing that privacy rules may change, even in established relationships such as those between parents and children, and the challenges and opportunities associated with such privacy rule change.

Same-sex couples' descriptions of their marriage or decision to marry as a contextual criterion for privacy rule change is consistent with CPM predictions about family communication and previous family communication research. As part of CPM, Petronio (2002, 2010) describes the ways in which changing connections between individuals and the family, such as marriages and divorces, lead to changes in privacy rules and boundaries. Research examining communication among in-laws and marital couples have shown the ways in which new marriages serve as a trigger and contextual factor for the changing of privacy rules for families and the turbulence often associated with such situations (Mikucki-Enyart, 2011; Serewicz & Canary, 2008). In showing that the introduction of same-sex marriage into a family also triggers the changing of privacy rules, this study provides further evidence of similarity between the relational experiences of same-sex and different-sex couples (e.g., Kurdek, 2000). At the same time, the accounts of couples who pointed to the existence of same-sex marriage itself as a contextual criteria for the changing of privacy rules in families highlight the significance of same-sex marriage not just as a shift in civil relationship recognition, but as a new way of understanding same-sex relationships within social networks.

Negotiating Sharing the News about Same-sex Couples' Marriages

The second theme to emerge from same-sex couples' descriptions of their interactions with family members about same-sex marriage illustrates how same-sex couples and their families negotiated sharing the news about the couples' marriages. One way that couples and their families attempted to deal with sharing the news about the couples' same-sex marriages was to try to coordinate sharing information about the marriage. According to CPM, people jointly manage collective boundaries regarding private information with others and these boundaries may vary in permeability (Petronio, 2002). This process of privacy boundary rule coordination for private information may be especially important in families because ties between family members are often expected to be stronger than those between other groups. By its very nature, civil marriage is a way for couples to share information about the existence of their relationship and their commitment to each other with their social network and society. Yet, civil marriage for same-sex couples is new and regionally limited. Therefore, the sharing of information about being or getting married may not be not as routinized for same-sex couples as for different-sex couples. Couples described how they and family members discussed how to share the news of their engagement or marriage, therefore explaining how boundary linkages regarding information about the same-sex marriage were coordinated. Many couples described consulting family members on how "traditional" information sharing about the marriage should be. For example, Mark and George involved Mark's parents in discussions of whether or not to place a wedding announcement in the newspaper. Some couples and family members, usually parents, decided whether or not to send formal engagement announcements and to whom to send such announcements together through direct discussions. Usually, when the decisions about whom and how to tell about the marriage were made jointly between the couple and family members the privacy boundary permeability was moderate to low. For example, Jess explains how her mother was involved in discussions about sharing information about her engagement to Sonya:

> Jess: We talked to my mom about telling my nieces and younger cousins. She felt some of them were too young to be told about a same-sex marriage.
> Sonya: We disagreed.
> Jess: Yeah, but we worked it out so that we told the kids together. We made sure my sister didn't tell them before we could all talk together about it. Mom was good with that.

Some couples directly told their family members about their engagement but did not involve their families in decisions about who else to tell and did not attempt to regulate with whom family members shared the news. In this way these couples allowed for higher privacy boundary permeability than other couples.

When they discussed how they and their families negotiated sharing news about their marriage, same-sex couples also described privacy turbulence regarding sharing news of the marriage. Privacy turbulence, also known as "boundary turbulence," is described by Petronio (2002, p. 177) as "asynchronicity in rule usage" that leads to conflict and miscommunication among people attempting to coordinate shared privacy boundaries. Privacy turbulence regarding sharing news of their same-sex marriage was discussed by many couples, especially involving asynchronicity in privacy boundary ownership. Couples described feeling upset because they had less control over the information about their marriage than they wanted due to disclosures made by family members. For example, Lucy described a problem with "ownership appropriation" (Petronio, 2002) involving her mother: "I was so mad at my mom when she told our old neighbors I was getting married. I wasn't going to because if they knew they would expect an invite." Other couples also explained turbulence relating to ownership and control of information. For example,

> Franklin: My sister tried to convince us to wait on telling my parents we got married. She kept saying things like 'we can do it when we are all ready.'
> Simon: The 'we' here is her and us!
> Franklin: Surprised us! We thought it was our marriage, our business.

The privacy turbulence discussed by couples reflected issues with ownership and control of information that may be common when any couple is sharing news of getting married, yet is simultaneously unique to same-sex couples whose marriages challenge heteronormative expectations (Oswald, Blume, & Marks, 2005). In her study of commitment ceremonies, Stiers (1999) demonstrated ways that same-sex couples incorporated heteronormative marriage traditions *and* made changes to expected marriage norms. Couples in my study were faced with not only negotiating who and how to tell about their marriage or engagement, but often did so with the added challenge of negotiating others' discomfort, uncertainty, and disapproval connected with their same-sex marriage.

Privacy dilemmas regarding identities were also described by same-sex couples as they discussed negotiating with their family members about sharing the news of their marriage. As Petronio (2002) explains, privacy dilemmas are always related to privacy turbulence resulting from trying to negotiate complex and often conflicting privacy management needs. Inherent in same-sex marriage is not only disclosure of the couples' relational status and commitment, but disclosure of the couples' GLBT sexual orientations and family members' status as someone with a GLBT relative. Thus, in disclosing that a same-sex couple has or is going to have a marriage, private information about people's identities, beyond marital status, may be revealed.

Some same-sex couples discussed how sharing information about their engagement and/or marriage involved negotiating privacy boundary linkages and often privacy turbulence related to revealing information about their sexual orientations. For some couples, discussing the decision to get married meant telling some family members that they were a romantic couple for the first time. In many cases, these discussions involved children. For example, Daphne explained, "I told my 7-year-old nephew that Velma and I were getting married. He looked confused and said, 'but you are girls.' I told him that some girls love girls, some boys love boys." Couples also discussed announcing their engagement to family members who they assumed knew they were romantic couple, but with whom it had not been explicitly discussed previously. For example, Tonya described telling her cousin that she and her partner were getting married and her cousin responding by saying, "I knew you were a couple, but wasn't sure if I was supposed to know." In addition to these coming out/same-sex marriage discussions linking privacy boundaries within families, couples also described similar discussions outside of the family exterior boundary involving friends of the family, neighbors, church members, and other extended social network members.

While some couples discussed how telling a person inside or outside the family involved a revelation of sexual orientation for them, it was common for couples to describe ways in which disclosing their same-sex marriage was a type of "coming out" for their family members who negotiated revealing that they had a GLBT family member. This family member "coming out" was associated with privacy turbulence relating to privacy boundary linkage, permeability, and ownership. Privacy turbulence erupted when family members would become upset that people (inside or outside the external family boundary) were told of the same-sex marriage because the family member associated a stigma with having a GLBT relative. In some cases, this privacy turbulence was most strongly an issue of privacy boundary linkage in that the family member wanted to limit the number and type of persons who knew about the marriage. Other descriptions of privacy turbulence centered on privacy boundary ownership and disagreements over who owned the information about the existence of the same-sex marriage. For example,

Jasper: My dad and I got in a huge fight one day and he said, 'You are going around telling people my private business.' I said, 'What f***ing business?' He said, 'That my son is gay.' I screamed, 'Dad, it's my marriage, my life, not yours.'

Jasper's example illustrates the crux of the turbulence over information ownership found in many of the couples' descriptions: the GLBT person sees the marriage information as belonging to him or her, while the family member sees the fact that they have a GLBT relative as belonging to him or her.

Participants also described cases of privacy turbulence rooted in disagreements about control of information. For example, Sandra stated, "Mimi's mom is an issue for us. She wants to be the one to tell the rest of the family about us getting married. It hurts us because we know she wants to be in charge because she is embarrassed." Finally, privacy turbulence was rooted in discordance around how permeable the exterior family privacy boundary should be. As illustrated by Elena, family members often wanted a less permeable boundary that would keep the information about the same-sex marriage in the family while couples wanted a more permeable boundary allowing their marriage to be public knowledge:

My mom kept saying, 'Why a big wedding? Keep it a small family affair.' She kept asking to remove people from the guest list until it was just family. We had a fight. She thought a small wedding would mean less people would have to know her daughter was married to a woman. Then, I was really upset.

Couples were often surprised by the privacy turbulence associated with disclosure of their same-sex marriage and by the "coming out" experienced by family members. For many couples, these turbulent discussions were their first inkling that their family member had not previously disclosed their relatives' sexual orientations and relationship status to others. An example can be found in Kellie's description, "My dad freaked about me getting married because he hadn't even told his brothers that I was gay. I thought they all knew!" Couples often described feeling betrayed by the closeted nature of their family members' previous approach to them and their relationship. As Foster explains, "I was hurt. I thought my brother was supportive of Gordon and I...he was until we were getting married and he couldn't explain him as my 'friend' anymore." Descriptions of family members as supportive of the relationship before the couple decided to get married, but being unsupportive of the decision to have a same-sex marriage, have also been found in previous studies (Lannutti 2007b, 2008).

Same-sex marriage, by being marriage, defies euphemistic explanations (such as they are friends or roommates) of the couples' relationships. As such, same-sex marriage challenges a family member's ability to remain closeted about their GLBT relative. Although much has been written about the coming out experiences of GLBT people (e.g., Savin-Williams, 2001) and the stigma and resulting negative outcomes GLBT people experience in relation to their identities (see Herek, 1998), little attention has been paid to the experiences of family members who disclose that they have a GLBT relative (D'Augelli, 2005). Schulman (2009) argues that for GLBT people coming out is a "process of self-interrogation in opposition to social expectation that has no parallel in heterosexual life" (p. 1). While the experiences of a family member who discloses that he or she has a GLBT relative may be qualitatively different than the coming out experience of the GLBT individual, the experiences share a common fear of, and sometimes experience of, social stigma and related stress (Beeler & DiProva, 1999; Crosbie-Burnett, Foster, Murray, & Bowen, 1996). Petronio (2002) explains that stigma risk can play an important role in an individual's deciding whether or not to disclose private information. However, this stigma is usually associated with information about one's own behavior or identity. This study emphasizes the importance of considering the secondary stigma that may be associated with revealing another person's stigmatized identity and one's association with that person.

Couples' descriptions of the privacy dilemmas regarding identities associated with same-sex marriage also highlight challenges and tensions around internal and external family privacy boundaries. As mentioned earlier, same-sex marriage served as a catalyst for more permeable internal and external family privacy boundaries for some couples and families, but for others, same-sex marriage caused or emphasized tensions around these boundaries. Couples' examples of parents who wanted to limit information about their marriage to "just family" or family members who wanted to exclude other family members from knowing about the marriage demonstrate the way that despite legal recognition, the marriages of same-sex couples may still be perceived as outside of the otherwise established family privacy rules. This difference in how same-sex couples are treated may lead to a sense of disconfirmation and rejection from family members, even when the family member otherwise expresses support to the couple for their relationship. Thus, the ways that internal and external family privacy boundaries are regulated in the same-sex marriage context may be particularly complex.

Negotiating Revealing and Concealing Couples' Relationship Details

The third theme to emerge from the same-sex couples' descriptions of discussing same-sex marriage with their families illustrates the ways couples negotiated revealing and concealing their relationship details with family members. Although all of the couples had established and ongoing relationships with some members of their own and their partners' families-of-origin before getting married or engaged, couples described ways that they experienced privacy boundary rule coordination and privacy turbulence regarding private information about their relationship in light of their marrying or deciding to marry. The new context created by the couples' same-sex marriage resulted in both increased disclosure and increased protection of private relationship information, often simultaneously, within the same family relationships. This dialectical nature of revealing and concealing private information within personal relationships is an assumption of CPM (Petronio, 2002) and widely discussed in the Communication literature (see Chapter 2; Baxter & Montgomery, 1996).

Same-sex couples described turbulence regarding when and how to share information about their relationship with family members that developed when they discussed their marriage with their families. Petronio (2002) explains that people rely on "privacy boundary linkage rules" to help them decide when and how to share personal information so that collective boundaries around that information may be formed. Two boundary linkage rules identified by Petronio (2002) were evident in couples' descriptions of their interactions with family members about their marriage. First, people try to time their disclosures to be most optimal and appropriate. For many couples, now that they were married or engaged, the time to reveal more details about their relationship to family members had come. As Cherie explained, "I guess it felt awkward to talk with our parents about our future plans about kids until we got married." Other couples discussed privacy turbulence related to timing of linkages resulting from waiting too long to share private information with family members. As illustrated by Joan,

> After we got married, I felt like we did a lot of 'going back and filling in' with April's sister. It felt right to let her know more details about us as a couple now, but it would have been less awkward, maybe less hurtful for her, if we told her along the way.

Second, Petronio (2002) describes how people may attempt to form privacy boundary linkages by acquiring private information through probing or questioning. Couples discussed how family members asked questions or hinted at questions about them as a couple, especially about the couples' plans regarding children, once they were married or engaged. As Megan explains, "As soon as we got engaged, our moms started asking if we were going to have kids. We have been together 4 years and they never asked until now!"

In addition to coordinating privacy boundary linkages in light of their marriage, same-sex couples also described coordinating privacy boundary permeability within families and between the family and non-family others now that they were married or engaged. Privacy boundary permeability refers to how much information flows over the boundary. For many couples, boundaries within the family become more permeable than they were before the couple was married or engaged. For example:

> Juli: I feel like once we were married, her family was much more open with me and we were much more open with them.
> Anna: What do you mean?
> Juli: Like at your sister's birthday party when we were all talking and your Mom told us about when she and your dad starting dating in high school and then everyone talked about when they were first getting together…us too.
> Anna: Yeah, but we knew that already.
> Juli: Not in that much detail. People really opened up. It's not like it was before.

Couples also described how they tried to maintain a less permeable internal boundary between them and their families once they got engaged or married. For example, Charlotte explained how she and her wife were careful to maintain a "sense of specialness and privacy" around some details of their relationship and their wedding itself while working with their families to plan their wedding.

Not all privacy boundary permeability coordination described was smooth. Couples described feeling "awkward" about keeping some details about their relationship private while other couples felt "frustrated" with the lack of sharing of personal information between them and their family members even though they were now married. As Ethan explained, "You would think in a family all couples would talk about themselves the same. Not in his family. They don't want to hear much about us, just the straight couples." Ethan's example serves as more evidence of same-sex couples, despite legal recognition, having internal family privacy boundaries applied to them in an atypical way.

Coordinating privacy boundary ownership and related privacy turbulence was also evident in couples' descriptions of their interactions with family members about their relationship. Some couples displayed what Petronio (2002) calls "fuzzy boundaries" as they discussed how they disagreed with each other about whether some information was personal, dyadic, or familial. As Candice and Stephanie illustrate:

> Candice: We had a few quarrels about telling my family too much.
> Stephanie: Like when you told your sister about us applying to adopt.
> Candice: Yes. I thought it was ok to tell my sister. It was a big reason we got married. But she wanted to wait until we were further in the process to tell the family.
> Stephanie: Not just the family. Anybody.

Other couples described how a part of being married was to have less control of their private information because they became a more regular topic of family gossip. For example, Gloria explained how her mother now included "daily updates" about her and her wife in her gossiping with Gloria's aunts although she did not before Gloria and her wife were married. For Gloria and many other participants, having less control over private information was the price paid for having greater acceptance and recognition within the family.

Married and engaged same-sex couples' discussions of privacy boundary coordination and privacy turbulence regarding private details of their relationship echoes research by Suter and colleagues (Suter, Bergen, Daas, & Durham, 2006; Suter & Daas, 2007) examining lesbian couples' management of public-private dialectical contradictions inherent in relationship rituals (such as anniversaries) and symbols (such as rings). Same-sex marriage provided a counterpoint to the heteronormativity that previously framed many couples' and families' boundary coordination regarding details about the couple and served as a trigger for adjustments in privacy boundary coordination and subsequent turbulence.

My study of the interactions between couples and their family-of-origin members about the couples' same-sex marriages illustrates the ways in which the introduction of same-sex marriage serves new context that affects and is affected by family communication. The couples' marriages served as a contextual criterion for shifts in privacy boundaries and a trigger for negotiations about how to manage privacy boundaries both within the family and between the family and their larger social network. Couples and their families negotiated how to share news of the couples' marriages and how to manage the couples' private information in the context of same-sex marriage. The study showed that same-sex marriage served as a means to share more information and grow closer for some families, while other same-sex couples and their family members were challenged by turbulence as they tried to negotiate privacy management related to same-sex marriage. Although the study focused on privacy management specifically, it suggests that many aspects of communication within families may be affected by and affect the couples' and family members' experiences of same-sex marriage. While my study focused on same-sex marriage as a new relational context for same-sex couples and their family-of-origin members, other research examines same-sex marriage and families created by same-sex couples.

Same-sex Marriage and Families Created by Same-sex Couples

There is an extensive body of research examining characteristics and experiences of same-sex couple headed families (see Goldberg, 2010). While it is not possible to review all of the literature on same-sex couple headed families here, there are important themes that emerge from this literature that are relevant to thinking about same-sex marriage and families created by same-sex couples.

Much of the existing research on same-sex couple headed families has focused on characteristics of children raised in these families. In 2005, the American Psychological Association (APA) produced a brief on gay and lesbian parenting (American Psychological Association, 2005). The APA, based on an extensive review of research, concluded that there was no evidence to suggest that gay and lesbian people were unfit parents and no evidence of significant disadvantages to children as a result of being raised by gay or lesbian parents (APA, 2005). Although the APA's conclusions about gay and lesbian parenting have met with some controversy (Amato, 2012; Eggebeen, 2012; Marks, 2012; Regnerus, 2012; Osborne, 2012), the APA's statement accurately reflects the majority of research comparing children raised by different-sex parents and children raised by same-sex parents which finds more similarities among these two sets of children than differences. However, the APA (2005) report also highlights one important difference in the experiences of children raised by different-sex parents and children raised by same-sex parents: children raised by same-sex parents often experience stigmatization and discrimination against their families because of their parents' sexual orientation. It is because of this discrimination and stigmatization that the American Academy of Pediatrics supports civil marriage for same-sex couples (Perrin, Siegel & Committee on Psychological Aspects of Child and Family Health, 2013). Specifically, the American Academy of Pediatrics has concluded that, "Marriage equality can help reduce social stigma faced by lesbian and gay parents and their children, thereby enhancing social stability, acceptance, and support" (Perrin et al., 2013, p. e1381).

While the American Psychological Association and the American Academy of Pediatrics have weighed in on the experiences and social status of families created by same-sex couples, further research has shown how same-sex marriage affects the way that families created by same-sex couples are perceived. Research indicates that same-sex couples who are co-parenting children are more likely to be recognized by others as a "family" than are same-sex couples who are not parents (Baxter et al., 2009). The presence of children may offset objections and challenges to a same-sex couple's identity and practice as a family (Koening Kellas & Suter, 2012). As discussed in Chapter 3, same-sex couples cite increased legal protection and social acceptance for having children or wanting to have children as attractions to same-sex marriage and as benefits of being legally married (Badgett, 2009; Hall, 2005; Ramos et al., 2009).

Research has also shown that same-sex couples believe that being married benefits their children. Ramos et al. (2009) report that 93% of married same-sex couples with children in their study believe that their children are happier and better off as a result of their marriage. Married same-sex couples with children also reported that their children felt more secure, have a greater sense of stability, and "saw their families as validated by society" because of their parents' same-sex marriage (Ramos et al., 2009, p. 1). But, how do the children of same-sex couples themselves describe their perceptions of same-sex marriage and same-sex marriage's role in their families' identities?

Research on the perceptions of same-sex marriage held by children of married same-sex couples is relatively scarce. Hall (2005) reported on interviews with children of same-sex parents married in Massachusetts. According to Hall (2005), the children of same-sex couples felt that that marriage equality for their parents and other same-sex couples was important and "right," but that the children viewed their parents' wedding ceremonies and parents' marriages themselves as more meaningful to their parents than to them. Goldberg and Kuvalanka (2012) interviewed adult children of GLBT individuals about their perspectives on same-sex marriage and found that their participants unequivocally supported same-sex marriage as a means for same-sex couples and their families to gain important legal rights, such as adoption rights and health care coverage. The children of GLBT people also cited symbolic benefits of same-sex marriage including making the relationships of same-sex couples and their families seem more "intelligible and real" (Goldberg & Kuvalanka, 2012, p. 45). Yet, one quarter of Goldberg and Kuvalanka's (2012) participants also mentioned some criticism of same-sex marriage or the fight for marriage equality while acknowledging the legal and symbolic benefits. Among the concerns about same-sex marriage and the fight for marriage equality mentioned by Goldberg and Kuvalanka's (2012) participants were suggestions that relationship termination may be more complicated after same-sex marriage and doubts about the high amount of energy and resources the GLBT community focused on marriage equality. Although limited, the research on the understanding of same-sex marriage held by children of same-sex couples suggests that they recognize same-sex marriage as a mechanism for helping to communicate a family's identity as a "legitimate" family.

Taken together, the research on families created by same-sex couples suggests that same-sex marriage may benefit these families. Same-sex marriage is a means to alleviate the discrimination and stigma faced by these families. Same-sex marriage may also help these families to clearly communicate their identity as a "legitimate" family to their social network and society in general. As such, same-sex marriage has civil, social, and communicative implications for families created by same-sex couples.

Same-sex Marriage Experiences of Understudied Members of the GLBT Community

If you are interested in learing more about same-sex relationships and perform a search for studies within the research literature, you will quickly discover that although researchers refer to the "GLBT" community, they often just include people who identify as gay or lesbian in their research samples and rarely include people who are bisexual and/or transgender among their participants. Further, these studies based on samples of gay men and lesbians tend to include groups of particpants who are mostly White, middle-class, urban, college-educated, and under the age of 50. Thus, much of what we know about same-sex relationships and the GBLT community is based on the experiences of only part of the community. The research literature examining same-sex marriage is still relatively new and limited, yet this growing body of research is vulnerable to the same lack of diversity that exists in the more general GLBT and same-sex relationship literatures. Given the lack of attention paid to certain segments of the GLBT community in the current research literature, I conducted two studies to attempt to learn more about the same-sex marriage experiences of some understudied members of the GLBT community. While these studies represent only one small piece of a research body that needs much more diversity and inclusiveness, the studies suggest that understudied members of the GLBT community may have unique experiences with legally recognized same-sex marriage that warrant futher research attention.

Bisexual-lesbian Couples' Same-sex Marriage Experiences

People who identify as bisexual are often challenged by both heterosexual and homosexual people (Mulick & Wright, 2002; Ochs, 1996). Negative at-titudes towards bisexual people often suggest that bisexuality is a phase, bisexual people are actually gay or lesbian, or bisexual people cannot commit to a relationship (Hutchins, 1996; Israel & Mohr, 2004). Although bi-sexual identities are recognized in the common vernacular of discussing the "GLBT" community, the uniqueness of bisexual identity when researching and discussing same-sex relationships is often ignored (Burleson, 2005; Hutchins, 1996).

In order to better understand the intersection of legally recognized same-sex marriage and issues related to bisexual identity, I conducted a study of married and engaged couples in which one partner identified as bi-sexual and the other partner identified as lesbian (see Lannutti, 2007b).[1] I chose to focus on bisexual-lesbian couples because research on identity poli-tics suggests that bisexual-lesbian couples may have relational experiences that are unique to cross-sexual orientation same-sex relationships between women. While negative attitudes toward bisexual people have been found among heterosexual and homosexual people (Hutchins, 1996; Israel & Mohr, 2004), Rust (1995, 2000) suggests that some lesbians' negative atti-tudes towards bisexual women are particularly complex due to women's po-litical struggles. According to Rust (2000), the "biphobia" displayed by some lesbians towards bisexual women includes two types of beliefs: "ex-planatory" beliefs that challenge the existence of bisexuality as a true sexual orientation, and "depoliticizing" beliefs that bisexual women are politically dangerous to lesbians because they lack loyalty to the lesbian community.

Given the larger social context of identity politics, my study examined the ways in which married or engaged bisexual-lesbian couples experienced the impact of their marriage or decision to marry on their romantic rela-tionships and their relationships with others. Participants discussed the im-pact of same-sex marriage on their lives along four distinct, but interconnected themes: their self-images, their romantic relationships, their relationships with social network members, and their relationships with the GLBT community.

Same-sex Marriage and Self-image among Bisexual-Lesbian Couples

The first theme that emerged from my interviews with bisexual-lesbian couples describes their perspectives on the impact of same-sex marriage on their views of themselves. First, many of the bisexual participants discussed how their decision to marry a female partner caused them to reflect on their own bisexual identity in the context of same-sex marriage, and they saw same-sex marriage as an affirmation of their bisexual identity. These partic-ipants saw the legal recognition of same-sex marriage as a sign of recogni-tion and acceptance for those who are not heterosexual, resulting in a sense of support for their bisexual identity. For example, "I wanted to get married because same-sex marriage isn't just for gay and lesbian people, it's for all of us who love a same-sex partner. It made me feel proud to be bi and with Valerie."

Other participants explained that being able to have the same legal recognition of their relationship with a woman as they could for a relationship with a man affirmed their bisexual identity by removing a barrier to their relational freedom. For example, "Now that I could marry a woman, I didn't feel like in being with a woman I had to give anything up anymore. I could be married and have everything I would want in a committed relationship." As another participant explained,

> I was so excited that marriage was being recognized for everybody. I mean, for me, being bi has always been about making my own choices and not having society or whatever make them for me. I could choose who to love. Now, I can choose who to marry.

The second way in which participants discussed the relationship between same-sex marriage and their self-images was by reflecting on what it meant to be (and have) a wife within the context of same-sex marriage. Some participants expressed excitement and comfort with the institution of marriage (e.g., "I always wanted to get married" and "We were already acting like we were married before it was legal"). Others discussed the ways in which they sought to find a fit between their self-image and their understanding of marriage. Echoing comments from participants in studies discussed in Chapters 2 and 3, many participants commented on their initial reluctance to getting married due to political and philosophical issues with the institution of marriage. For example:

> Marie: We were both nervous about getting married. We didn't want to seem like we were acting straight. And we didn't want to be our parents.
> Rebecca: Yeah, marriage is so mainstream. I never wanted to get married even when I thought I was straight. It just wasn't me.
> Marie: And we both hated the history of marriage. Women being property and all that. We couldn't see ourselves as wives.
> Rebecca: We had to think about it in a different way.

Many participants explained that they dealt with misgivings about heteronormative marriage by defining or redefining marriage-related terms in a way that fit better with their self-concepts. For example, participants avoided the term "wife" and instead used terms such as "spouse" and "partner" to refer to each other. Others resisted negative images of wives in marriages by co-opting traditional language through tongue-in-cheek references to each other as "my bitch" or "my old lady." Participants also spoke of their definition of marriage versus what they perceived as a heteronormative definition of marriage. For example,

> Carol: I'd been married to a man before. He was really controlling, and I guess I thought that was what marriage was like. I couldn't be that person again, so we talked about it.
> Diane: We talked about it a lot.
> Carol: Yeah, and I realized that it wasn't that I wasn't the marriage-type, I just wasn't the controlling marriage-type.
> Diane: Right. We had to be sure to have a marriage that fit who we were. For me, too.

Same-sex Marriage and Bisexual-Lesbian Couples' Romantic Relationship

The second theme that emerged from my interviews with bisexual-lesbian couples was the effect of same-sex on the couples' relationship with each other. All of the couples expressed some way in which same-sex marriage improved or strengthened their romantic relationship. Many couples discussed feeling that their relationship was stronger because it now had legal protections. For example, "Getting married helped us because we didn't have to worry anymore about what would happen if something horrible happened to one of us. I know she will be taken care of now because of the legal protections." Another participant stated, "I think because we are more legally secure now, we feel more secure in our relationship."

Other couples expressed the ways in which same-sex marriage contributed to a closer emotional bond between them. Many couples expressed greater feelings of love as a result of getting married. For example, "Obviously, we loved each other or we wouldn't have gotten married. But actually being married has made our love deeper I think." Another woman stated, "Having made those vows in front of our family and friends made me realize how much I really cared for her and how much I really did want to spend my life with her."

Couples also discussed how same-sex marriage strengthened their relationship by creating the opportunity to reflect on their relational goals and values with one another. For example:

> Marianne: We didn't just get married right away because we could. We really thought and talked about it.
> Elaine: It was a serious decision for us. We talked about what we thought was important in a relationship. What our strengths and weaknesses were. We hadn't done that much before.
> Marianne: Well, we didn't have intense conversations like that before thinking about getting married.
> Elaine: That's true. It really helped make us closer. And feel more confident about marriage.

The discussion of relational values and goals was sometimes explicitly related to one partner's bisexual identity. For example,

> When we talked about getting married, I made it really clear to Patty that even though I would always think of myself as bi, I was making a lifelong monogamous commitment to her and I expected the same from her.

Another bisexual participant expressed how marriage strengthened their relationship by showing her partner the depth of her commitment:

> Right after we got married, Marcie told me that she felt a lot happier in our relationship. She confessed that she worried deep down that I wouldn't be able to ever fully commit to her because I was bi. Getting married made her forget that stupid idea.

Although all of the couples discussed how same-sex marriage made their relationship stronger, many also discussed how same-sex marriage challenged their relationship.

Some couples discussed the stress that was introduced into their relationship through either their marriage decision process or planning their weddings. While the discussions about getting married were a means to a stronger emotional bond for some couples, others expressed hurt feelings and relational distancing during their marriage decision-making process. For example:

> Emma: It was kind of a struggle for us to decide to get married. I wanted to right away, but she was unsure.
> Sarah: Well, I was sure I loved her, but I wasn't sure if we were ready for marriage. I didn't want to do it just because it was legal.
> Emma: Neither did I. But, I really wanted to marry her because I loved her and I thought the protections would help us.
> Sarah: We fought about it. I actually moved out for a short time.
> Emma: It was horrible. But, we worked it out. We both needed to grow-up I think.

Other couples discussed challenges in deciding the terms of their marriage. For example, "I wanted us to be married, but have an open marriage. She wanted no parts of that." Another participant explained, "We were all excited about getting married, but when it came down to pooling our financial resources, I became less sure. We almost broke-up over money before I realized how untrusting and unfair I was being."

In addition to challenges to the relationship presented as part of the marriage decision-making process, couples also discussed how planning their wedding ceremonies introduced stress into their relationships. For example:

> Grace: I had been married to a man before. I didn't want anything that was like that wedding.

> Maria: But, I wanted some of the traditional things. Like a formal reception and stuff like that. I didn't see why her straight wedding before should mean we couldn't have some of those nice things, too.

Many couples expressed problems with planning their wedding ceremonies because they lacked support from their families-of-origin. For example, "I really didn't want to have a big wedding at first because I knew my parents wouldn't come. In the end, we had the wedding, but it was bittersweet for me."

The idea that same-sex marriage would help to strengthen same-sex relationships, especially through legal protection, is consistent with previous research discussed in Chapter 2. However, the present data are also consistent with research discussed in Chapters 2 and 3 in that same-sex marriage is also seen as challenging to couples. The couples interviewed for this study echo struggles with the symbolism and logistics of marriage discussed by GLBT people who chose to marry and those who chose not to marry in Chapter 3. Suter et al. (2006) discussed how lesbian couples may struggle with the public-private dialectic in their commitment ceremonies because members of the couples' families-of-origin are unsupportive of the relationship. Those concerns were shared by some bisexual-lesbian couples who participated in my study and same-sex couples who participated in studies discussed in Chapters 3 and 4. The relationship between same-sex marriage, the bisexual-lesbian couples, and their families and friends is explored further next.

Same-sex Marriage, Bisexual-Lesbian Couples, and Social Networks

The third theme that emerged from my interviews with bisexual-lesbian couples describes the influence of same-sex marriage on couples' relationships with their social network members. First, all of the couples discussed how the legal recognition of same-sex marriage or their specific decision to marry affected their relationships with their families-of-origin. As with participants in studies in Chapters 3 and 4, the most frequently discussed family-of-origin members were the couples' parents. Some couples discussed the support they felt from their families for same-sex marriage in general. For example:

> Jody: The whole marriage debate really helped my relationship with my parents. They were so upset at how the anti-marriage people acted.
> Cynthia: Her parents never were really supportive of us before.
> Jody: They weren't unsupportive. It's more like they didn't take our relationship very seriously before I guess.
> Cynthia: But they got really involved in the fight against the anti-marriage amendments.

Other couples explained the support they felt from family members for their marriage specifically. For example, "My parents were happy we could get married because it made us so happy." Some participants explained how their parents were surprised by their decision to marry because of their bisexual identities, but were supportive of the decision nonetheless. For example:

> When I told my mom that Robyn and I were getting married, I wasn't sure how she was going to react. But, she just started laughing and saying she was glad I was going to finally going to marry somebody. I asked her why she said that, and it turns out she was worried that because I was bi I was never going to have a secure lifelong relationship with someone. I have no idea why she thought that. It's not like I even dated around that much!

Although some couples described how one partner's bisexual identity was associated with surprised, yet supportive reactions to their marriage plans from family members, others described family members who were both surprised and unsupportive. Participants explained how their family members, particularly parents, seemed to view their bisexuality as reason to hope that they would someday choose to marry a man. For example:

> Alex: My parents, especially my mom, lost it when I told them we were engaged.
> Piper: It was a nightmare. They were never really happy about us, but they were coping. But, this did it for them.
> Alex: I was surprised. When they finally spoke to me, they told me that they thought that being with Piper was a phase…that I would find a man someday.
> Piper: Imagine, I'm a 4 year phase!
> Alex: I asked them why after all this time they would think that, and they said 'you call yourself bi, not a lesbian.' Anyway, they are still upset. They say they won't come to the wedding.

Another participant explained,

> My sister was totally against us getting married. She could accept me dating a woman, but not marrying one. We had this fight and she said that I've dated men before and that I should wait to marry a man.

For other couples, families were simply unsupportive of their marriage because it was a same-sex marriage, regardless of the participants' individual sexual orientations. For example, "My parents were so embarrassed that I was marrying a woman. They had told people we were roommates all this time." Participants also mentioned that their families were unsupportive of their marriage for religious reasons.

In my study of attractions and obstacles to same-sex marriage discussed in Chapter 3, lack of family approval was the most frequently identified obstacle to marriage. Although the struggle for same-sex couples to gain acceptance and support from families-of-origin is a commonly reported stressor (e.g., Kurdek & Schmitt, 1987; Rostosky et al., 2004; Smith & Brown, 1997) and has been discussed in detail in Chapter 4, the interviews with bisexual-lesbian couples highlight the role that misperceptions about bisexuality play in increasing this stress. Family members' attitudes reflect belief that bisexual women cannot fully commit to another woman. Ironically, some families hold on to this belief as a "ray of hope" that their bisexual family member may reconnect to the heterosexual world, while ignoring the fact that believing in this myth creates greater stress and distance in their relationship with her.

Some bisexual-lesbian couples also described how same-sex marriage impacted their relationship with their friends, specifically their lesbian friends. Some couples described the ways in which their lesbian friends pressured them to consider marriage. For example,

> As soon as it became clear we could get married legally, it seemed like all of our lesbian friends started asking us when we were getting married. And they persisted. It became annoying after a while because we wanted to really think about it seriously.

Another couple describes how a lesbian friend seemed to challenge one partner's bisexuality while pressuring them to marry:

> Nikki: This one friend, Michelle, she was kind of over supportive.
> Helen: I wouldn't describe it as supportive. She was almost like a bully about it. She kept saying 'you should get married.' Then, when we would say we were thinking about it, she would say 'Well, why not, Helen? If you can be bi and live with a woman, you can be bi and marry a woman, can't you?'
> Nikki: It bothered Helen…throwing the bi thing at her like it was something wrong. I think she was just being protective of me, though. She wanted Helen to make a commitment to me.
> Helen: Fine. But I never said I wouldn't marry you and it had nothing to do with being bi. Michelle was really pushy and rude. I mean, I did marry you. I wanted to.

Other couples described how some lesbian friends attempted to assert their influence on the ways in which the couples defined their marriages and themselves. Some couples described how a lesbian friend asked specific questions about the terms of their marriage. For example, "My friend Susan, she kept asking, 'Is it a monogamous marriage? She won't be able to date men will she?'" Many lesbian friends seemed to take the marriage as a sign that the bisexual partner no longer identified as bisexual. For example,

> Deciding to get married actually started some fights with our friends, our lesbian friends. They would make a joke like, 'Well, I guess Natalie grew out of that bi thing, huh?' and eventually we had to come back at them.

Another couple explained:

> Blair: Sometimes when we told people we were getting married, they would say, 'So, you're giving up on guys for good?' or something like that. I got really mad, especially when lesbian friends would say it. It was like they had won a game or something.
> Jo: It was annoying because she had never been with a guy while with me. We were exclusive. She was making a commitment to me, not 'women.'
> Blair: It was really because they resented me being bi I think. It made me sorry I ever labeled myself as anything.

The pressure felt by bisexual-lesbian couples to marry and to define the terms of their marriage in ways that their lesbian friends approved of reflects the tension between lesbian and bisexual women described by Rust (1995; 2000). Couples' descriptions of how lesbian friends sought for signs of loyalty to the lesbian partner, a proxy for the lesbian community, through a monogamous marriage is reflective of Rust's (2000) "depoliticizing" aspect of biphobia. "Explanatory" biphobia (Rust, 2000) is evident in lesbian friends' direct challenges to their friends' bisexual identity now that she had decided to marry a same-sex partner.

Same-sex Marriage, Bisexual-Lesbian Couples, and the GLBT Community

The fourth theme that emerged during my interviews with bisexual-lesbian couples describes how same-sex marriage influenced the couples' relationships with the larger GLBT community. First, some couples described feeling a stronger sense of belonging to the GLBT community because of legally recognized same-sex marriage. Many couples described feeling more a part of the community as the community struggled to maintain their marriage rights. Although Massachusetts, the state where the couples resided, began recognizing same-sex marriage in May 2004, there were several attempts at overturning these rights. At the same time, there was the threat of federal legislation against same-sex marriage. Some participants described a renewed sense of belonging with the community as it continued its political struggle for same-sex marriage. For example,

> We got really involved in all the political stuff to protect marriage. Going to the state house, stuff like that. It reminded me how great the queer community can be, and how much I had drifted away from queer events.

Other participants described feeling a part of the GLBT community for the first time as a result of the struggle for same-sex marriage. For example,

I'd never been into any type of community action stuff. I mean, I'm not the kind of person who wears t-shirts about being bi or anything. Everyone got together to fight to protect it…it didn't matter to me whether I belonged before.

In addition to feeling an increased sense of belonging to the GLBT community because of the political struggle over same-sex marriage, couples discussed feeling more united with the community because of their marriage itself. Several couples described a sense of "being counted" as part of the community through their marriage. For example, "Because we are married we are officially registered as a same-sex couple. It made us realize that our marriage isn't just about us, it's a part of something bigger that couldn't happen before the law changed." Other couples felt that in getting married, they were more accepted as a couple by the larger GLBT community. For example, "There is kind of a pride in the married couples, I think. Like, our gay friends, they are always introducing us as their 'married' friends and people are instantly excited about that."

While many couples expressed feeling a stronger sense of belonging to the GLBT community, other couples explained how the political struggle over same-sex marriage made them feel that their relationship was invisible in the GLBT community. Couples discussed how getting married made them little more than a statistic to the GLBT community. For example, "I think that to some people, all that matters is that as many people as possible get married and stay married. Who cares who you are…we need numbers!" Other couples discussed how their relationship became defined by the community as a "lesbian marriage" and erased the uniqueness of their relationship, especially one partner's bisexuality. One couple's discussion shows how frustrated this sense invisibility may become:

> Martina: All you ever hear about is 'lesbian and gay marriages.' It makes me mad that we don't use the term 'same-sex marriage.' I mean, it's like we don't want to complicate things or something.
> Ellen: It shouldn't really matter I guess. But it seems like how we see ourselves doesn't matter right now.
> Martina: I just didn't want to hear about our 'lesbian wedding' anymore. Everybody, even our very gay florist who we've known for years kept calling it a 'lesbian wedding.' Sometimes I wanted to yell, 'This is not a lesbian wedding!' but then again, do labels really matter? It only matters that we are married and can stay married. So, we put up with it.

Same-sex marriage affected the intersection between the couples and the larger GLBT community in two ways. As discussed by GLBT community members in Chapter 2, the bisexual-lesbian couples described feeling a part of a united GLBT community struggling to protect the civil institution of same-sex marriage. Some bisexual-lesbian couples also felt that by specifically expressing their commitment through marriage, they had an opportunity to be affirmed by the GLBT community. In contrast, other couples explained how expressing their commitment through same-sex marriage increased their sense of being ignored by the GLBT community because same-sex marriage cloaked the uniqueness of their relationship and identities. As such, same-sex marriage served as another example of the way that bisexual experiences and concerns become invisible as they are subsumed under the GLBT banner (see Hutchins, 1996).

My study showed that bisexual-lesbian couples experienced same-sex marriage in many ways that are similar to other same-sex couples. The bisexual-lesbian couples interviewed for this study, like other GLBT people and same-sex couples discussed throughout this book, also experienced same-sex marriage as a complex, and often contradictory, context that both benefited and challenged their primary relationship and their relationships with their social networks and the larger GLBT community. However, my study also showed several unique same-sex marriage experiences of bisexual-lesbian couples. For example, participants explained how lesbian friends displayed biphobia in discussing the couples' marriage and marriage-decision process and the way in which getting married seemed to cloak the couple's identity as a *bisexual*-lesbian couple within the GLBT community.

While my study describes same-sex marriage experiences of bisexual-lesbian couples, an important limitation of this study should be noted. This study focused on only one type of couple in which a bisexual person may experience same-sex marriage. Previous research has found that bisexual men and women significantly differ in their attitudes toward same-sex marriage from each other and from their gay and lesbian counterparts (Galupo & Pearl, 2007). The experiences of the bisexual-lesbian couples interviewed for this study may differ, for example, from the experiences of male-male cross-sexual orientation couples. Future research should examine the ways in which legally recognized same-sex marriage influences the relational experiences of bisexual-gay male couples, and the same-sex marriage experiences of bisexual-bisexual same-sex couples.

Same-sex Marriage Experiences of Older Same-sex Couples

Like bisexual individuals, older GLBT people receive relatively little research attention, especially when one considers research on same-sex marriage. The lack of research on older same-sex couples in the same-sex marriage literature is consistent with a problematic tendency to exclude older people from consideration in the GLBT research literature (Berger & Kelly, 1996; Gabbay & Wahler, 2002). Yet, given the lived history of older GLBT people and the impact that history is likely to have on their relational lives, it is reasonable to expect that the same-sex marriage experiences of older GLBT people may be different than those of younger GLBT people.

The past half-century has been a time of tremendous change in the legal and social status of lesbian, gay, bisexual, transgendered and queer (GLBT) Americans (for reviews see Cook-Daniels, 2007, and Marcus, 2002). For older GLBT individuals who have experienced coming-of-age and coming out during such turbulent times, these social and political changes have most likely had significant effects on their self-concepts, social network relationships, and romantic relationships (Kimmel, Rose, Orel, & Greene, 2006). For example, a female-female couple in their mid-60s may have come to better understand their sexual orientation during the women's liberation movement of the 1970s which was often conflicted about the role of lesbians and bisexual women within the movement (Jay, 1999). They may have struggled to come out during the turbulent 1980s in which a Gay Rights movement fueled by the AIDS crisis was in conflict with the conservative political climate of the Regan era (Schulman, 1994). The couple may have become more public about their relationships and experienced workplace discrimination based on their sexual orientation during the 1990s. At the same time, the 1990s politics of visibility may also have exposed their family and friends to more positive and diverse images of the GLBT community in the media and influenced them to be more accepting of the women as a couple (Streitmatter, 2008). The couples' experiences of their own identities and their relationships may have been influenced by political and social changes regarding homosexuality in the United States. Therefore, the relational lives of older GLBT individuals need to be considered within the context of their unique historical perspective.

While some older individuals have been included in studies examining legal marriage for same-sex couples, the mean age of participants in most same-sex marriage studies has been in the 30s and 40s (e.g., Badgett, 2009; Lannutti, 2007b). One significant discussion of same-sex marriage and the perspective of an older generation of GLBT people can be found in a study by Porche and Purvin (2008). In their study of the meaning of same-sex marriage for long-term same-sex couples (together for over 20 years), Porche and Purvin (2008) included three couples in their 50s and three couples in their 60s. Porche and Purvin (2008) suggest that older same-sex couples are more likely to view marriage as unnecessary and instead see other markers of commitment, such as joint home ownership, as significant. This finding is consistent with Recheck et al.'s (2009) contention that long-term same-sex couples do not follow normative commitment-making trajectories. Porsche and Purvin (2008) also suggest that older same-sex couples may be more resistant to same-sex marriage if the couple lacks connection to the larger GLBT community.

While Porche and Purvin's (2008) observations offer initial insight into the marriage experiences of some older same-sex couples, their study is limited because it is based on so few interviews with older couples. To fill this gap in the same-sex marriage literature, I decided to conduct a study focusing on the same-sex marriage experiences of older same-sex couples. I interviewed 36 older (defined as each member of the couple being over 55 years of age) married (22 couples) and unmarried (14 couples) same-sex couples residing in Massachusetts after same-sex marriages had been recognized in the state (see Lannutti, 2011a).[2] I spoke with the couples about their reactions to legally recognized same-sex marriage and the surrounding debates, how legally recognized same-sex marriage has impacted their relationship with one another and their social networks, and about their own decisions to marry or not. Older same-sex couples discussed their experiences with legally recognized same-sex marriage along three distinct, yet interconnected themes: an increased sense of security, an increased sense of recognition, and their misgivings about same-sex marriage.

Like Porsche and Purvin (2008) and Recheck et al. (2009), my study of the same-sex marriage experiences of older couples is framed by a life course perspective. Elder (1994) describes a life course perspective in which the influence of social change on people's lives and relationships is examined. Among the principles of a life course perspective is consideration of historical events in people's lives, attention to the timing of social change within a person's life, the ways in which one person's life is linked to others, and human agency and decision making (Elder, 1994).

Same-sex Marriage, Older Couples, and Increased Sense of Security

All of the married older same-sex couples whom I interviewed discussed experiencing an increased sense of security as a result of getting married. In contrast, non-married older couples did not mention security in their discussion of the impact of same-sex marriage on their lives. The first type of increased sense of security discussed by the married couples related to finances. Although many couples made joint financial plans and arrangements before same-sex marriage was recognized, the legal recognition provided by same-sex marriage bolstered their sense of shared financial security. This increased sense of financial security was especially emphasized in regard to financial considerations in the event of one partner's disability or death. For example:

> Brooks: Having that piece of paper saying we are married just like everybody else who is married in MA makes me feel like we can finally relax about Charlie or I being taken care of in terms of money and the house if something happened to one of us. I mean it would be too hard for someone to come in and take those benefits away from one of us now.

Second, the married older couples discussed how same-sex marriage was a means of ensuring that spouses would be able to make medical decisions for one another and for providing health benefits for spouses that may have been previously unavailable before same-sex marriage. This gave them an increased sense of medical security. The concern around making proxy health decisions for one's partner was explained by Amy and Emily:

> Amy: One thing that I worry less about now that we are married is making decisions for each other in the hospital or something like that.
> Emily: Me, too. I mean, our doctors know us and know we are a couple. But now nobody can argue or hassle us in an emergency with nurses and doctors we don't know.
> Amy: We know we can take care of each other now no matter what.

Other couples discussed same-sex marriage as a means to extend health care coverage to a spouse that was not available outside of marriage. Many employer health plans do not cover "civil" or "domestic" partners, but do cover "spouses." Therefore, same-sex marriage allowed many older same-sex couples the opportunity to include a partner in their health coverage for the first time, therefore increasing their sense of medically related security.

The senses of increased financial and medical security from having legal recognition for their relationship suggest that same-sex marriage may be a means of alleviating some of the major challenges faced by older same-sex couples. Studies have shown that older same-sex couples who have not had the opportunity to legalize their relationship may face greater levels of financial uncertainty, especially in retirement, than may older different-sex couples (Riggle et al., 2006; Riggle, Rostosky, Prather, 2006). Without legal recognition for their relationship, older same-sex couples may also face more difficulties when interacting with the medical establishment than may different-sex couples because same-sex couples may not be recognized as health care proxies for each other (Blevins & Werth, 2006). While younger same-sex couples discussed in Chapter 3 also discussed financial protections as an attraction to same-sex marriage, such protections may be particularly important to older couples for whom issues such as shared retirement benefits are of pressing salience. In other words, same-sex marriage may provide increased financial and medical security to older same-sex couples at a time in their lives when they need it the most. In this sense, same-sex marriage may be a practical step to lessening the tangible negative effects of heterosexism in the lives of older same-sex couples and may help balance the resource inequality between different-sex and same-sex older couples discussed by Barker, Herdt, and de Vries (2006) and Hunter (2005).

Older married same-sex couples also discussed a third type of security increased by same-sex marriage: relational security. Although the average relationship length for older couples I interviewed was 18.44 years, couples described feeling more secure in their relationships as a result of getting married. Some partners discussed feeling an increased or renewed sense of love between them as a result of getting married. As explained by Dorothy, "Getting married after all this time together was like a gift that let us stop and remember what a special thing we have together." Other married couples expressed a deeper sense of security due to the traditional aspects associated with marriage, such as the spousal titles of "husband" or "wife" or wedding rings. As an illustration:

> Jordan: There is something really nice about saying 'my husband' without any irony to it.
> Paul: We never really used that term like some other couples did... you know, before marriage was legal. But there is something really solid to it. Comforting.
> Jordan: 'Husband' just seems like a better word. Stronger. More permanent. I love to say it and hear him say it really.

A life course perspective, as described by Elder (1994), emphasizes the importance of considering social change as it affects the relationships among people. The increased sense of relational security as a result of same-sex marriage discussed here by older same-sex couples echoed that discussed by younger same-sex couples discussed in Chapter 3 and interviewed by Badgett (2009). The sense of increased relational security experienced by older couples as a result of same-sex marriage suggests that even couples who have been in a committed relationship for long periods of time may relationally benefit from formalizing their commitment with same-sex marriage.

Same-sex Marriage, Older Couples, and Increased Sense of Recognition

The second theme that emerged from older same-sex couples' discussions of their experiences with same-sex marriage is an increased sense of recognition for their relationships. Unlike the theme of increased security, which was discussed by married couples only, both married and unmarried couples described how same-sex marriage added to their sense of being recognized as a legitimate couple. The couples discussed increased senses of personal and political recognition illustrating the significance of same-sex marriage as it relates to the links between the couples and their social networks and the place of same-sex marriage within the unique historical context of the couples' lives.

The couples' discussion of an increased sense of personal recognition, as with the increased sense of relational security discussed by married couples above, illustrates the value of considering social change as it affects relationships among people (Elder, 1994). Married couples expressed an increased sense of recognition for their relationship from people close to them, such as friends, and those with whom they are less close, such as neighbors or fellow church members. In this way, the social change of same-sex marriage can be seen as directly affecting the social ties between older same-sex couples and their immediate and extended social networks. Although older married couples did feel an increased sense of recognition, note that a sense of increased personal recognition from families was less prominent among older couples than in previous studies about the effects of same-sex marriage discussed in Chapters 2 and 3. Several explanations are possible for this difference in perceived personal recognition between older couples and younger couples discussed in Chapters 2 and 3. First, it may be that older couples have fewer family-of-origin members in their lives (e.g., parents are deceased). Additionally, older couples' relationships with their families-of-origin may have been established long ago as accepting or rejecting, therefore lessening the current impact of same-sex marriage on such relationships.

Some non-married older couples also expressed feeling an increased sense of recognition for their relationships as a result of the existence of legally recognized same-sex marriage. As one couple explained:

> Chuck: One thing is that we seem to be more noticed as a couple.
> Scott: Some people have started pointing out how long we've been together and asking us what we think about marriage.
> Chuck: Like all the marriage stuff in the news has made people focus on us as a couple more.

The recognition of same-sex marriage and the surrounding debates has emphasized the relationship of both married and non-married couples in the eyes of others and led to an increased sense of recognition for same-sex romantic relationships.

An important aspect of the increased sense of personal recognition present in the older couples' experiences of same-sex marriage not found in previous studies centers on the issue of widowhood. For older couples, same-sex marriage has occurred in a time in their lives when widowhood is becoming a more salient concern. The older couples' discussions of widowhood and the benefit of increased recognition due to same-sex marriage illustrate the life course principle of the importance of considering the timing of social change within a person's life (Elder, 1994). Many couples expressed concerns about what would happen to a partner if the other died and the ways in which same-sex marriage contributed to alleviating that concern. This concern about widowhood went beyond the type of financial security discussed above, and included a focus on the social aspects of losing a spouse. By increasing the sense of recognition for the couple, same-sex marriage was seen as a way to increase social support for a widowed partner. For example:

> Martha: I like that everyone knows we are married, really married. So, if something happens to me, everyone will have to see how hard that is on Rosie.
> Rosie: It's kind of sad but true. It seems like before people could just trick themselves into seeing us as close friends or roomies or something. We are a married couple now.

Other couples reflected on the social uncertainty they had witnessed when other long-term same-sex couples experienced a death of one partner. As an illustration:

> Tegan: Sometimes people don't act right when someone dies. They act like the relationship wasn't what it was. Or they are uncomfortable or confused. You don't get treated like a widow. Like something less.
> Sara: Right. It's so unfair. It has happened so many times, especially with other family members. They don't take it as serious as if a straight couple had it happen.
> Tegan: But being married makes people see it. Your wife has died. Your wife.

Couples' concerns with the issue of widowhood, both in practical and personal terms, reflects the difficulties often experienced by GLBT individuals after the death of a long-term partner. Without relationship institutionalization, the death of a long-term same-sex partner has often lacked the social recognition and support provided to those who have lost a different-sex spouse (Hunter, 2005; Slater, 1995). While advanced planning for finances and health care by same-sex couples outside of same-sex marriage may help to alleviate concerns about the material implications of a partner's death (Riggle et al., 2006; Riggle, Rostosky, Prather, 2006), the couples in my study suggested that same-sex marriage is a means to assure that the emotional and social implications of a partner's death will be recognized and therefore more likely to gain the social support needed for survivors. Thus, having same-sex marriage available in late adulthood when concerns about widowhood become more salient may increase the significance of same-sex marriage for older same-sex couples.

In addition to an increased sense of personal recognition for their relationships due to same-sex marriage, older couples also expressed an increased sense of political recognition for themselves, the GLBT community, and same-sex relationships. Like GLBT people surveyed about the potential effects of same-sex marriage in Chapter 2, older married and unmarried couples universally viewed same-sex marriage as a sign of political success for the GLBT community and as a sign of societal progress. Older same-sex couples discussed the political recognition represented by same-sex marriage as it related to their lived experiences of the changing social and political status of the GLBT community in the United States. Many couples viewed same-sex marriage as a significant benchmark in the struggle to end discrimination against GLBT people. As Pat stated, "[Same-sex marriage] is huge. I am so happy to see gay people standing up for themselves and their relationships and not being shoved right back down." Others viewed the political recognition associated with same-sex marriage as the commencement of the GLBT civil rights movement. An example was provided by Ruth: "[Same-sex marriage] is coming full circle for me. It's finally winning rights for lesbians and gays." Many participants expressed a sense of awe in seeing same-sex marriage come to pass in their lifetime. For example:

> Brian: I get choked up to think about it sometimes. I can remember when you had to hide or be afraid of getting arrested, beat up…
> Justin: I was even arrested once.
> Brian: …you could have been fired. I used to think it was amazing to be able to tell people we were together without worry. But, to be married to the man I love!

Unmarried couples who have chosen not to marry also discussed the increased sense of political recognition and societal acceptance resulting from the existence of legally recognized same-sex marriage. For example:

> Emmett: It is wonderful to have that option for those who want it. I never thought I would live to see such a thing.
> Ted: I loved the photos in the news of gay couples lining up to get married the night you could in Cambridge.
> Emmett: It was the kind of moment in history you just have to reflect on and smile.

The participants' discussions of their experiences of same-sex marriage as an indicator of increased political recognition should be considered with reference to Elder's (1994) idea of lives within historical times. As noted previously, the participants in this study came-of-age and came out during a time of rapid and turbulent change in the social and political status of GLBT Americans. Thus, their experiences of same-sex marriage should be considered within the context of that unique historical perspective rather than understood as an isolated reaction to political events from 2004 to the present. In the case of increased political recognition, older same-sex couples saw same-sex marriage as a positive, and in some cases culminating, event for themselves and the GLBT community. Next, the theme of misgivings about marriage illustrates the ways in which some participants' historical perspective leads to a more negative view of same-sex marriage.

Same-sex Marriage, Older Couples, and Misgivings about Same-sex Marriage

While the older GLBT people I interviewed saw some positive aspects of same-sex marriage, even if they did not feel it personally benefitted them, some older GLBT people also discussed misgivings about same-sex marriage. Both married and unmarried couples described the ways in which they found same-sex marriage to be challenging. Older same-sex couples' misgivings about same-sex marriage included concerns about mainstreaming, viewing same-sex marriage as dangerous, and finding same-sex marriage unnecessary. Although many of these misgivings about same-sex marriage were also discussed in Chapter 3 as concerns expressed by same-sex couples who chose to not marry, the older couples' misgivings illustrate the influence of older same-sex couples' unique historical perspective on their experiences of same-sex marriage, how some couples' agency in choosing or not choosing same-sex marriage is constrained, and how same-sex marriage is related to some couples' misgivings about presenting and defining their relationship to others.

Older couples' first type of misgiving about same-sex marriage focused on couples' concerns that same-sex marriage was a means of mainstreaming same-sex relationships and the GLBT community as a whole. Some couples expressed concerns that same-sex marriage was an attempt to "act like straights." Others discussed same-sex marriage as a type of begging for acceptance or validation. An example was provided by Anthony: "Fighting for marriage and getting married is like saying that we need approval from the straight community to be seen as valid couples. We have to use their terms to be accepted." The issue of seeing same-sex marriage as an attempt at mainstreaming same-sex couples and GLBT people is not unique to older couples. Similar concerns that same-sex marriage would mask the uniqueness of same-sex relationships and suggest that same-sex relationships are not legitimate outside of a traditionally heterosexual institution such as civil marriage were expressed by GLBT people surveyed about the perceived effects of same-sex marriage in Chapter 2 and reflect long-standing debates within the GLBT community regarding same-sex marriage or marriage-like recognition (Badgett, 2009; Pinello, 2006; Yep, Lovaas & Elia , 2003). Still, concerns about mainstreaming for older same-sex couples are likely rooted in historical experience. Tensions about which images of GLBT life and which examples of GLBT relationships are seen by and presented by the GLBT community as most positive existed throughout the GLBT liberation movement of the 1970s and 1980s as well as the politics of visibility of the 1990s. These tensions are reflected in the older couples' views of same-sex marriage as a potentially mainstreaming tool.

The second type of misgiving about marriage discussed by older same-sex couples was defined by the idea that same-sex marriage was dangerous or threatening to couples and individuals. Same-sex marriage was seen as a type of visibility for couples and individuals that might lead to threats to one's property or personal safety. For example, one man expressed concerns that same-sex marriage put a "target" on gay and lesbian people and that getting married was simply "asking for trouble." Another couple expressed concerns about same-sex marriage and harassment:

> Dawn: We thought about getting married, but we tend to keep our private life private.
> Researcher: How does not getting married keep your private life private?
> Dawn: If you get married, it's a public statement. For everyone. Like registering yourself as gay down at city hall.
> Corey: We just have had trouble in the past when people we don't really know find out about us. You see those nuts with the 'God hates gay' signs down at the state house. We'd just as soon keep our life private and just between those we are close to. Not be bothered by stupid folks that are just ignorant.

None of the couples who discussed same-sex marriage as dangerous decided to marry. This suggests that even in a location where same-sex marriage is recognized, older same-sex couples may still be wary of harassment and discrimination against GLBT individuals. In context, this is understandable. The lived history of the older same-sex couples in this study includes many high-profile cases of harassment, discrimination, and violence against GLBT people. As Cook-Daniels (2008) explains, a gay American man in his 60s today would have a living memory of the pre-Stonewall-era discrimination against GLBT people, homosexuality being defined as a mental disorder by the American Psychological Association, government and healthcare discrimination during the advent of the AIDS crisis, and the murder of Matthew Shepard. In addition, many participants have personally experienced harassment, discrimination, and violence due to their sexual orientation. The participants' experiences of same-sex marriage as potentially dangerous illustrate the impact of their historical perspective on their current experience with same-sex marriage (DiPlacido, 1998; Grossman, 2006; Meyer, 2003). The view of same-sex marriage as dangerous goes beyond concerns about marriage itself and also reflects concerns about negative consequences of the social and political debates over same-sex marriage. These concerns are consistent with previous studies showing that debates surrounding same-sex marriage and the passage of marriage amendments limiting marriage to different-sex couples in some locations has had negative psychological consequences for GLBT individuals such as increases in feelings of minority stress (Riggle, Rostosky, & Horne, 2009; Rostosky, Riggle, Horne, & Miller, 2009).

The third type of misgiving about same-sex marriage discussed by older couples had to do with the idea of same-sex marriage being unnecessary. First, same-sex marriage was described as unnecessary because it was redundant with arrangements or ceremonies that couples already had. For example:

> Bette: We just felt like getting married, legally, was not important for us. We went to a lawyer many, many years ago and had papers made up about the condo, money, wills. All that.
> Tina: Yeah, at our age we were really careful about that and that kind of stuff is really the big benefit of marriage anyway. So, we don't need it.

The explanation that same-sex marriage is not needed because it is redundant with financial and legal arrangements already made by the couple is consistent with reasons not to marry offered by same-sex couples who chose to not marry discussed in Chapter 3 and participants in a study by Porche and Purvin (2008). The experience of same-sex marriage as redundant with other financial and legal arrangements illustrates the ways in which a couple's choice to have a legally recognized marriage is constrained. Like many long-term same-sex couples, participants sought legal protection for each other and their relationship through alternative arrangements to marriage because same-sex marriage was not available to them when such protections were needed and desired (Recheck, Elliott, & Umberson, 2009). Now that the social change of legally recognized same-sex marriage has occurred for these couples, they are choosing not to marry in part because they want to maintain or protect previous legal and financial arrangements.

Other couples explained how their previous commitment ceremonies made same-sex marriage unnecessary. As an illustration:

> Rita: To us, we really have been married for almost 10 years already. We got married, it has always been real to us.
> Bonnie: Yeah, our commitment ceremony was beautiful. We don't need to get married again. We are married.
> Researcher: So, you don't feel that the legal status of marriage is something you need?
> Rita: Well, it feels like getting married again now would make it seem that we really haven't been married all this time, and we have been.

For many couples who engaged in commitment ceremonies or other commitment rituals before same-sex marriage was legally recognized, engaging in same-sex marriage is viewed as renewing their marriages at best or invalidating their previous ceremonies at worst. This underscores the significance of commitment ceremonies for same-sex couples when same-sex marriage is not available (Stiers, 1999). Thus, same-sex marriage presented a challenge to some older same-sex couples' ways of defining and presenting their relationship to their social network before same-sex marriage was available. Some participants chose to remain with their previous way of defining and presenting their relationship, while some couples chose same-sex marriage despite their feelings that it was mostly unnecessary. In these cases, the same-sex marriage was often described as "a little something extra" or "following through" on previous commitments rather than a new relational turning point or commitment event as described by Schecter et al. (2008). Elder's (1994) consideration of the time in a person's life in which social change occurs is also relevant to understanding the participant's view of same-sex marriage as unnecessarily redundant with previous financial and legal arrangements or with previous expressions of commitment. Perhaps if these older couples had the option of legally recognized same-sex marriage earlier in their lives when they needed and wanted such arrangements and expressions of commitment, they would have chosen same-sex marriage over other alternatives.

The older couples interviewed did not all choose to engage in same-sex marriage, but they all confronted the decision to marry or not. When considering a major social change like same-sex marriage from a life course perspective, it is important to recognize the value of human agency as couples negotiate the role same-sex marriage will play in their relational lives (Elder, 1994). The older couples who chose same-sex marriage saw it as means to increase financial and medical security for them and their partners. Others saw same-sex marriage as unnecessary because of previously established financial and long-term planning and/or because of the importance of previous commitment ceremonies as an enactment of commitment outside of same-sex marriage. Thus, the couples' agency in choosing or not choosing same-sex marriage was influenced by previous decisions regarding commitment and the time in which same-sex marriage occurred in their lives (Elder, 1994). Whether older same-sex couples decided to marry or not, their decision-making process about same-sex marriage reflected the importance of establishing legal protections for long-term same-sex relationships. The experiences of older same-sex couples illustrate the intersection between legal and political context and a person's and couples' lifespan and their influence on relational experiences and expression of commitment.

The Need to Understand the Diversity of Same-sex Marriage Experiences

My studies of bisexual-lesbian couples' and older same-sex couples' marriage experiences are examples of studies that are needed to fill the gap regarding the underrepresentation of diverse groups within the same-sex marriage literature. In her discussion of intersectionality in social research, McCall (2005) urges researchers to refrain from dissecting the individual social groups to which people belong to better understand their experiences, but instead to explore the intersection of those social identities to better understand the experiences of social groups. While researchers should be cautious about pigeon-holing the experiences of various groups when exploring same-sex marriage, it is impossible to truly consider the intersectionality of experience without seeking out more diverse samples in our studies of same-sex marriage and honoring the unique perspectives gained from multiple-minority group membership.

More research is needed to better understand the same-sex marriage experiences of GLBT people who belong to diverse racial and ethnic groups. There is a dearth of research focusing on the same-sex marriage experiences of African American, Latino American, and Asian American GLBT people. Although a few studies have focused on same-sex marriage experiences of members of these groups, such as Khan's (2011) study of South Asian American same-sex weddings, much more research is needed to better understand the same-sex marriage experiences of members of these groups. Otherwise, we are left to infer information from bits and pieces of studies focusing on same-sex marriage that may include relatively few non-White participants. A research report published by the PEW Research Center for the People and the Press in June 2013 suggests that while support for same-sex marriage among non-GLBT Americans has grown since 2001, African Americans (39%) still support same-sex marriage at a lesser rate than do White Americans (51%) and Hispanic Americans (60%) (PEW Research Center, 2013). We can extrapolate that GLBT people with families and social networks that are predominantly African American may experience more resistance to their same-sex marriages than may other GLBT people. The reasons for African American's relatively low support of same-sex marriage are unclear. Some research suggests that religion has an especially significant influence on attitudes toward same-sex marriage among Latino and African American non-GLBT people in the U.S. (Ellison, Acevado, Ramos-Wada, 2011; Sherkat, de Vries, & Creck, 2010). Moore (2011) highlights the importance of attention to the way that GLBT people who are also members of racial and/or ethnic minorities are positioned to have the influence of diverse social ideologies and norms influence their experience of same-sex relationships and marriage. To follow Moore's (2011) call, more research that delves deeply into the same-sex marriage experiences of GLBT people who belong to diverse racial and ethnic groups is needed.

There is also a need for more research so that we may gain a better understanding of the same-sex marriage experiences of those who do not identify as gay or lesbian. I discussed the need for more studies of bisexual individuals' experiences of same-sex marriage above. There is also a need for more research examining the same-sex marriage experiences of transgender individuals. Research focusing on the experiences of transgender individuals in same-sex marriages or transgender attitudes toward same-sex marriage is virtually nonexistent. Although some studies of same-sex marriage include a few transgender individuals in their samples, such as I did in my research discussed in Chapter 2, transgender experiences regarding same-sex marriage are likely to be complex and require more research attention to be understood. Transgender individuals challenge norms and beliefs about the nature of gender roles, gender identity, and sexual orientation which may result in complex relationships with the GLBT community and society in general and a unique perspective on same-sex marriage and its surrounding debates (Nagoshi, Brzuzy, & Terrell, 2012). Further, the application of various marriage laws to transgender individuals is complex and often unclear (see Taylor, 2007). For example, in some states a transgender man may marry a woman as long as his sex has been legally recognized to be male, while in other states he would still only be allowed to marry a person who was born male, and yet if he were to marry in a state that allowed same-sex marriage than he might be free to marry a male or female partner. Further, research on the communicative struggles and experiences of families when a member of that family is trans-identified suggests that a transgender person's social network members may struggle with meaning-making around the transgender person's identity (Norwood, 2012a, 2012b). We might expect that a transgender person's communication with his or her social network about same-sex marriage may differ from that between a gay, lesbian or bisexual person and his or her social network. More research is needed to explore this communication.

Additionally, Scherrer (2010) points out the need to consider asexual individuals' relationships in the context of legally recognized same-sex marriage. Scherrer (2008) describes the ways in which asexual individuals, or those who do not experience sexual attraction or desire, are similar to GLBT individuals in that they are members of a sexual minority, experience a "coming out" process, often rely on the internet for community connection, and have been classified as problematic in the history of medical discourse. Given these similarities, Scherrer (2010) argues that asexual individuals should be considered in the same-sex marriage debate and that asexuality serves to highlight some of the limitations of same-sex marriage and our way of discussion relationships in general.

Research focusing on the same-sex marriage experiences of non-White and non-gay or lesbian people suggests that the intersectionality of multiple identities may influence the same-sex marriage experiences of these diverse groups and their social networks. However, this research is very limited. Further, there are other types of diversity, including age, income, religion, and region that need further exploration. Thus, the existing literature leads to many more questions which call for more diversity in future same-sex marriage research.

CHAPTER SIX

When Banns Are Banned:
Experiences of Same-sex Marriage Prohibitions

Thus far, this book has focused on the experiences of American same-sex couples who have the option of legally recognized marriage. Yet, at the time this book was written, the majority of U.S. states (38) had either amended their state constitutions or passed legislation to prohibit the legal recognition of same-sex marriage (see *Marriage*, n.d.). As discussed in Chapter 2, same-sex marriage is a new type of relational context for same-sex couples in states that allow same-sex marriage and those that have banned same-sex marriage. The political battles for and against same-sex marriage and the dynamic changes in relationship recognition for same-sex couples have consequences for GLBT individuals, same-sex couples, and their social networks across the United States. Yet, most of the research on same-sex marriage has focused on legal recognition. This chapter focuses on experiences of same-sex marriage prohibitions of GLBT individuals, same-sex couples, and their social networks.

The research available on the social and psychological consequences of marriage restrictions has identified consequences for GLBT people and their social networks (Horne, Rostosky, & Riggle, 2011; Maisel & Fingerhut, 2011; Riggle, Rostosky, & Horne, 2009; Rostosky, Riggle, Horne, Denton, & Huellemeier, 2010). Riggle et al. (2009) examined the effects of the passages of marriage-restricting amendments in U.S. states in 2006 through a national survey and found that GLBT individuals were exposed to more negative messages about themselves and their relationships during the campaigns for marriage restrictions and experienced increases in negative psychological effects. Maisel and Fingerhut (2011) found that exposure to anti-same-sex-marriage messages during the campaign leading up to the passage of California's Proposition 8 banning same-sex marriage increased negative emotions experienced by GLBT people and often negatively impacted the social relationships of GLBT people. More specifically, Maisel and Fingerhut (2011) found that GLBT people reported heightened tension and conflict in their romantic relationships about involvement in campaigns related to Proposition 8 and marriage.

Extending the effects of marriage bans on GLBT people's social networks, Arm, Horne, and Levitt (2009) and Horne et al. (2011) found that family members of GLBT people had negative experiences relating to an amendment banning same-sex marriage in their state. Family members of GLBT people reported greater negative affect and greater exposure to negative messages about GLBT people than family members of GLBT people who lived in a state that did not pass a same-sex marriage ban (Horne et al., 2011). While Horne et al. (2011) found that the stress experienced by GLBT people in a state that passed a same-sex marriage ban was greater than the stress experienced by their family members, their results highlight the impact of the struggle for and against same-sex marriage on the social networks of GLBT people.

Yet, the research on the effects of same-sex marriage bans suggests that that the social and psychological consequences of marriage amendments and other legal restrictions on the lives of GLBT people and their social networks are complex and somewhat paradoxical (Maisel & Fingerhut, 2011; Riggle et al., 2009; Rostosky et al., 2010). Maisel and Fingerhut (2011) report that GLBT people reported some positive affect, such as pride and support, and a strengthening of personal relationships as a result of the struggle over California's Proposition 8. The introduction of same-sex marriage bans has also lead to GLBT individuals' greater engagement with the political process and greater political determination and sense of empowerment (Oswald & Kuvlanka, 2008; Riggle et al., 2009; Rostosky et al., 2010). Yet, Levitt et al. (2009) found that GLBT individuals facing marriage bans struggled with a balance between involvement in advocacy and self-protective withdrawal from engagement with the issues. This mix of positive and negative consequences of the introduction of same-sex marriage bans experienced by GLBT people echoes Russell's (2000) findings in her study of the psychological consequences of the passage of Colorado's anti-gay amendment in 1992.

Communication about Marriage Amendments: Same-sex Couples and Their Extended Social Networks

The previous studies examining the experiences of same-sex marriage bans by GLBT people and their social networks served as a springboard for my study of experiences of marriage amendments. Russell's (2000) study shows the stress and resilience associated with legislation that discriminates against GLBT people, but is not a specific study of the effects of relationship recognition restrictions and may have limited application to understanding the current relationship recognition context for same-sex couples. Riggle et al. (2009) specifically examined the effects of relationship recognition restricting amendments on GLBT people, but the survey format of their study did not provide for more detailed descriptions of the impact of the amendments on the social aspects of GLBT lives. Horne et al. (2011) provided insight into the impact of marriage amendments on GLBT individuals and their family members, but does not extend to other parts of the social network. Therefore, I conducted a study of the effects of marriage amendments limiting marriage to that between one man and one woman on an understudied aspect of same-sex couples' social lives (see Lannutti, 2011b).[1] The social consequences of marriage amendments examined in my study are those that can be observed in the interactions between same-sex couple members and members of their extended social networks. Extended social network members are people who are part of one's social network, such as work colleagues, team members, and casual friends, but are not considered to be close friends or family members.

As discussed in Chapter 1, Communication scholars have argued that interactions, especially our everyday interactions, are central to building and maintaining not only our social worlds, but also our identities and understanding of self (see Tracy, 2002, for review). Thus, to understand the social consequences of political action such as restrictive marriage amendments, one place to look is the interactions that people have with their social network members regarding the amendments. People's understanding of themselves and their social world as affected by the marriage amendments will be reflected in such interactions.

Social networks are complex and ubiquitous aspects of our lives, and attempts to study them have resulted in a variety of frameworks for understanding social networks and relationships within them. For example, scholars have conceptualized and examined social network density, overlap, distance, and contact (see Parks, 2007, for overview). My study relies on the concept of the "consequential stranger" in our social networks as described by Blau and Fingerman (2009). Blau and Fingerman argue that peripheral members of our social networks, those with whom we may have both direct contact (one to one interaction) and distant contact (contact through a mutual third party) without forming an emotionally close personal relationship, are essential and influential parts of our social lives. This conceptualization of consequential strangers, people whom I refer to as extended social network members to avoid the lack of direct contact implied by the term "stranger," as critical in our social lives is echoed by Christakis and Fowler (2009). Christakis and Fowler highlight the reciprocal socially supportive and persuasive abilities of extended social network members on one another.

Interactions with extended social network members were chosen as a location for examining the social consequences of marriage amendments for two reasons. First, a person's conception of "society" may be greatly influenced by interactions with extended social network members. Blau and Fingerman (2009) explain that those with whom we have seemingly casual interactions shape our understanding of our communities and our places within those communities. Christakis and Fowler (2009) point out that even interactions removed by three degrees of social distance (friends of friends of friends) can influence us and shape our view of social norms. In this way, extended social network members are on the border of "people we know" and "people in general" and interactions in this borderland may be illustrative of the ways that same-sex couples experience marriage amendments' impact on their social worlds. At the same time, the experiences of same-sex couples as they are impacted by marriage amendments may influence how couples' extended social network members perceive and act in relation to marriage amendments.

Second, extended social network members provide important resources for individuals and couples. Blau and Fingerman (2009) point out the ways in which acquaintances, neighbors, and colleagues create a web of social connections that can be relied upon for both material and social support at key points in our lives without the daily relational maintenance behavior typically associated with close personal relationships (see, Dindia, 2000, for overview). Parks (2006) explicates the ways in which social networks form a type of structural support for couple commitment. Same-sex couples in states with marriage amendments on the ballot may find themselves in acute need of the material and social support of their extended social network. As discussed by Ghavami and Johnson (2011) and Russell (2011), same-sex couples are a minority who rely on majority and other minority members as allies in legal battles. After a marriage amendment is passed, the interaction between a same-sex couple and their social network may be especially salient in how the couple understands their commitment in the face of new marriage restrictions.

All of the couples[2] who were interviewed for my study engaged in interactions with extended social network members regarding the marriage amendments in their state either during the month before the election or during the month after the amendment ballot measure passed. Four themes describing the interactions among the members of the same-sex couples and people in their extended social network regarding the marriage amendments emerged. The four themes are: coming out, social support, solidarity, and disconfirmation.

Coming Out to Extended Social Network Members

The first theme to emerge from the same-sex couples' descriptions of their interactions with extended social network members regarding their state's marriage amendment is coming out. Thirty-nine percent of those I interviewed described coming out during an interaction with an extended social network member. Coming out describes an interaction in which the GLBT person revealed his or her sexual orientation to the social network member through an explicit statement.

Many of the GLBT people I interviewed described coming out in these discussions as uneventful, as if describing a basic demographic fact about oneself. For example, Alice describes coming out to a friend of a friend while discussing the marriage amendments during a break in a shopping trip with a small group:

> Alice: So we decided to have lunch and I ended up sitting next to Shane, who I only met once or twice before. We got to talking about the election and the amendment. Shane asked what I thought about it and I said I found it really offensive. She asked why and I told her because I'm a lesbian and I've been with my girlfriend for 5 years and we were just like any other couple. She then asked a bunch of questions about me and Dana.
> Researcher: How did you feel about telling Shane you were a lesbian and about your relationship?
> Alice: Oh, nothing really. It's not a big deal or anything.

For others, coming out during discussions about the marriage amendments was more emotionally challenging. They describe feeling nervous, uncomfortable, or angry about coming out during their discussions. For example, Elton described coming out during an interaction with a neighbor while discussing the marriage amendments at a party:

> Elton: I was at this neighborhood get together and a guy from down the street brought up the amendment. This was about 3 weeks after the election. I couldn't tell his position on it. But, I don't know, I just decided to tell him. About me. I said you do know we're gay right. He said no. Kind of surprised maybe.
> Researcher: Why do you think you wanted to tell him about you?
> Elton: I don't know. I guess I wanted to make it clear who he was talking to before he went on with his opinion. It felt really kind of awkward. I guess I was mad or upset. I didn't want to have to share personal stuff with this guy but I didn't want to hear anti-gay stuff at that time either.

Even though the GLBT people I interviewed had both neutral and negative emotions about coming out during interactions regarding marriage amendments, none reported directly negative reactions to their coming out from social network members. Reactions of extended social network members to coming out statements were described as neutral or supportive only.

Coming out during discussions of marriage amendments is a type of self-disclosure worthy of discussion for several reasons. My participants' coming out during discussions about the marriage amendments highlights the interaction between communication with social network members and identity (Tracy, 2002). This coming out behavior suggests that one consequence of the marriage amendments is to increase the salience of GLBT individuals' identities as sexual minorities and their motivation to share that identity more widely by coming out to extended social network members.

Coming out, both as a process and as a type of self-disclosive statement, has received much research attention (see Hunter, 2007, for overview). Many researchers examine coming out in the context of a psychological and social process of accepting, adjusting to, and sharing one's sexual identity (e.g., Iasenza, Colucci, & Rothberg, 1996). Yet, coming out also has an important place in the political lives of GLBT individuals and the GLBT community. The concept of GLBT visibility is predicated on the belief that if more GLBT people identified themselves through coming out to more and more people, then eventually members of the larger society would realize both their own connections to GLBT people and the pervasiveness of GLBT people in society (Walters, 2001). In this way, GLBT visibility as a strategy depends on the contact hypothesis (Allport, 1954) which argues that members of different groups could reduce prejudice by getting to know each other better (see Brown, 1995, for overview). Yet, the contact hypothesis has been widely criticized as an unsuccessful strategy for reducing prejudice because prejudice-reducing contact seems to be contingent on a set of facilitative conditions such as cooperative independence and shared goals between members of the opposing groups that are inherently unrealistic in situations of inequality (see Rubin & Lannutti, 2001). Strategies based on the contact hypothesis have also been criticized for placing disproportionate emotional burdens on minority groups and for primarily benefiting dominant groups (Bar & Eady, 1998). The potential dangers of coming out in the context of same-sex marriage perceived by older same-sex couples in Chapter 5 and GLBT participants in Chapter 2 add further weight to criticism of visibility as a strategy.

It is important to consider participants' coming out disclosures to extended social network members during interactions regarding marriage amendments in the context of GLBT visibility and the contact hypothesis. Although participants did not indicate that they came out to extended network members as an explicit political strategy, the underlying principles of the contact hypothesis seem to be at work in many of their descriptions of the interactions. For example, Serena described coming out to another player during a bowling league match as something that she "felt was right so that he could get who the amendment was really about." Although no participant described a negative response to his or her coming out, many did describe having their own negative emotional reactions to coming out during the interactions about marriage amendments. This negative emotion is the type of burdensome consequence of the contact hypothesis critiqued by Bar and Eady (1998). However, a larger concern may be the ineffectiveness of increased GLBT visibility in the marriage recognition struggle. Despite the individual coming out behavior typical of the participants in this study and increased media visibility for GLBT people in the United States (Walters, 2001), to date, 38 U.S. states have enacted amendments to their state constitutions limiting marriage to one man and one woman (*Marriage*, n.d.).

The implications of coming out during a discussion of marriage amendments are mixed. On one hand, the potential benefits, both on the individual and community levels, of coming out to extended network members during discussions about marriage amendments may be outweighed by negative emotional consequences and limited effectiveness. On the other hand, Blau and Fingerman's (2009) concept of the consequential stranger suggests that coming out in these interactions may have powerful and persuasive effects that, although difficult to measure directly, may contribute to a reduction of prejudice against GLBT people and decrease in support of marriage amendments. Christakis and Fowler (2009) offer a useful perspective on the potential effectiveness of coming out as a tool in decreasing support for marriage amendments in their "three degrees of influence rule" of social networks. Building on Milgram's well-known six degrees of separation concept for the social world (see Travers & Milgram, 1969), Christakis and Fowler (2009) argue that one can influence ideas and actions in a social network to three degrees of social distance (e.g., a friend of a friend of a friend), but not beyond. This three degree rule would suggest that the influential power of explicit coming out statements may be limited to the receiver of that disclosure and people in two more degrees of distance from the GLBT individual at most.

Social Support from Extended Social Network Members

The second theme to emerge from the same-sex couples' descriptions of their interactions with extended social network members about marriage amendments is social support. Forty-eight percent of the participants described socially supportive interactions with extended social network members. One type of social support found in interactions about marriage amendments between participants and extended social network members is sympathy. Sympathetic interactions are those in which extended social network members acknowledge the emotional experience of the participant. GLBT people described sympathetic interactions both before and after the election in which the amendments passed. Sympathetic interactions before the election focused on anxiety or hope. For example, Ernie and Bert explain an interaction with a casual acquaintance before the election:

> Ernie: We saw this guy we know through Bert's former boss. We bumped into him. He was asking how we were feeling about the election coming...
> Bert: About the marriage measure. I said we were feeling nervous. That it was going to make it.
> Ernie: Right. He said he could only imagine how it would feel if he felt people were voting on his relationship. Would be uncomfortable.
> Bert: He's straight.
> Ernie: Yeah. He seemed to get why we were nervous.

Other couples described how extended social network members encouraged them to "stay hopeful" or "keep faith" even though polls were indicating support for the amendment.

Sympathetic interactions after the marriage amendments were centered on emotions of disappointment, anger, and sadness. Social network members acknowledged couples' emotions during the interaction and usually offered condolences. Kermit and Jim described an acquaintance's condolence expression:

> Kermit: We had brunch with some people a few weeks after the election. A woman I know from work who is a friend of a friend was there. She came up to us when we got there...
> Jim: Yeah, she really made a point of it. We don't know her well, so it was nice really.
> Kermit: She came up and asked how we were feeling about the ballot passing. We talked about being upset, of course. She said how sorry she was that it had happened.
> Jim: She was really nice.

Same-sex couples also discussed social support in the interactions among same-sex couple members and their extended social networks in terms of listening. Participants described the ways in which social network members allowed and encouraged them to talk about the experiences of the marriage amendments. For example, Audre described her interaction with a yoga classmate:

> Audre: I was at the gym after class and we got to talking. We sometimes did so I know about her kids and she knows about me and Adrienne. Just basics. Anyway, after the marriage thing happened we had this interesting conversation. She brought it up, but we actually got to talking so we went to coffee. Never did that before. She really listened to me. She wanted to hear how it felt for me.
> Researcher: How did that conversation make you feel?

Audre: You know, I think about it a lot. I think it was important for me to talk about it with someone who was a good listener. It's like it didn't really affect her, but it did in that she cared how it affected me, or people like me. Nice, you know?

Many couples echoed Audre's idea of the importance of being listened to and the connection that it seemed to create between them and the extended social network member. Same-sex couples also commonly described listening accompanied with offers of additional general social support. For example, social network members are often described as offering to "be there for" the couple.

The same-sex couples' descriptions of socially supportive interactions with extended social network members regarding marriage amendments highlight one of the important functions of social networks in our lives. Blau and Fingerman's (2009) argument that one role of consequential strangers in our lives is to provide social support is evident in the couples' descriptions of the sympathy and listening enacted by extended social network members. One limitation of my study is that it does not provide a comparison of the quality of social support received from extended social network members. Instead, my study provides a more macro level description of the socially supportive function of social networks (Cunningham & Barbee, 2000), and, in doing so, suggests that even casual connections may be an important source of social support for same-sex couples experiencing the stress and other negative psychological effects of marriage amendments described in other research (Levitt et al., 2009; Maisel & Fingerhut, 2011; Riggle et al., 2009; Rostosky et al., 2010). As in other research, my study suggests that anti-gay legislation may have some positive social consequence (Maisel & Fingerhut, 2011; Riggle et al., 2009; Rostosky et al., 2010; Russell, 2000). The couples' experiences of social support were a positive social consequence of the marriage amendment experience. However, this positive consequence should be considered in context: if same-sex couple members were not experiencing the negative effects of the marriage amendments and their surrounding debates, they would not have been in such acute need for support from extended social network members.

Solidarity between Same-sex Couples and Extended Social Network Members

The third theme to emerge from the same-sex couples' descriptions of their interactions with extended social network members regarding marriage amendments was solidarity. Solidarity is related to, but distinct from, social support because solidarity is defined by a sense of shared purpose. In other words, social support is an acknowledgment of someone's position, whereas solidarity is joining their position. Because all of the couples I interviewed were opposed to the marriage amendment in their state, solidarity is defined as sharing in the couples' purpose of opposing the marriage amendment. Twenty-eight percent of couples described solidarity in their discussions with extended social network members regarding marriage amendments.

First, same-sex couples described "solidarity of belief" in their interactions in which extended social network members expressed agreement with the couples' beliefs in opposition to marriage amendments. In nearly all interactions containing solidarity of belief, social network members first addressed the marriage amendment issue and volunteered solidarity of belief unsolicited. For example, one couple describes an interaction with a friend of a friend about pro-amendment advertising:

> Matt: We had a talk with this woman who knows our friend Andy.
> John: Yeah, at the store. She said hi and then we got to talking. Election was close so it came up.
> Matt: She wanted us to know that she thought some of the ads on TV were awful. Wrong.
> John: We agreed. Obviously.

Some couples described interactions in which they were solicited for information about the amendments by network members who already seemed in opposition to the amendments. For example,

> Leslie: This woman at work. She's in another department, but I see her at big meetings. She came up to me after a meeting and asked if we could chat. It was funny.
> Tara: Is this the 'honey' woman?
> Leslie: Yeah. She said it in this funny way. She said, 'Honey, this marriage business is all over the place. I know you have a partner. So, honey, tell me what I should know.'
> Tara: You are probably the only dyke she knows.
> Leslie: Probably. Anyway, I kind of was confused. I asked what she meant. She basically thought the amendments were wrong but wanted a list of reasons why. It was a good conversation actually.
> Researcher: So, you got the impression she was already against the amendment before speaking to you?
> Leslie: Yeah, she was. But it was like she wanted evidence from a real lesbian or something.

In addition to solidarity of belief, same-sex couples also described "solidarity of action" in which extended social network members and same-sex couple members discussed agreement about activities in opposition to the marriage amendments. The most commonly discussed solidarity action is voting against the amendment. However, other solidarity activities, such as posting political signs and volunteer work, were also discussed. For example, Tammy describes an interaction with a store owner about posting signs regarding the marriage amendment:

> Tammy: I went down to this cheese shop. Well, they have specialty foods. More than just cheese. We go in there a lot. Anyway, they had signs in the window from a group. You know, saying 'don't vote for the amendment.' The owner was in and we've chatted a few times in the store before.
> Violet: About cheese. And, not other stuff really.
> Tammy: Right, so this was different. About the sign and stuff. We said thanks for posting them and she talked about being happy to do that and about how some local church people were boycotting her, the store, but she didn't care.

Same-sex couples expressed positive outcomes of discussions with extended social network members in which solidarity of belief or action was expressed. These positive outcomes included feelings of acceptance and increased feelings of support for not only their position on the amendments, but for their relationship and identities as GLBT individuals. The solidarity of belief and action evident in the interactions between same-sex couple members and extended social network members are illustrative of the political power of social networks described by Christakis and Fowler (2009). Although the couples and the members of their social network joined in solidarity with them did not succeed politically, the solidarity showed the way that social networks are a source of political influence and material support in political campaigns. The findings on solidarity also highlight the political dependency of sexual minorities and the need for allies from the heterosexual majority (Russell, 2011) and other minority groups (Ghavami & Johnson, 2011). This solidarity may also be seen as providing a more specific form of social support. Maisel and Fingerhut (2011) found that GLBT individuals identified solidarity of action as a sometimes surprising, but positive, outcome of a same-sex marriage restriction ballot initiative. In expressing and acting in political solidarity with same-sex couples, members of their extended social network were providing not only political backing against the amendments but confirming support for participants as a couple and as GLBT individuals.

Disconfirmation from Extended Social Network Members

The fourth theme to emerge from the same-sex couples' descriptions of their interactions with extended social network members about marriage amendments was disconfirmation. Disconfirming communication is that which devalues a person's significance. Although only 11% of the participants described disconfirming interactions, the experiences of these interactions were described as intense, upsetting, and disturbing.

One type of disconfirmation described by same-sex couples was condemnation from extended social network members. In these condemning interactions, extended social network members explicitly expressed strong disapproval of the couple and often suggested that the couple was worthy of punishment. For example, Janice and Paige describe an interaction with a neighbor:

> Janice: Oh my god, we have this horrible neighbor. We live on a cul de sac so we all see each other all the time. Say hi. She puts this sign on her lawn supporting the marriage ban.
> Paige: So rude. But, we don't say anything because it's a free country, right? But we complain about it when we talk to our friends next door.
> Janice: Made fun of it really. Yeah, but, I don't know, I guess it got back to her. So, we are getting stuff out of the car one day and she comes over. To the drive. Unreal.
> Researcher: What happened?
> Paige: She starts saying that she has to support the ban because of her church. She says that she prays for us.
> Janice: Yeah, but not in a, like, a nice way. There was more to it...
> Paige: Yeah, she basically says how we are going to hell and she prays for us because of that. Awful. We have to live across from this crazy woman.

Many couples I interviewed described being surprised by condemning interactions. For example, Gerry described being "shocked" that a co-worker spoke about "gays trying ruin marriage" in his presence at a lunch meeting. All couples who described a condemning interaction described negative emotional consequences as a result of the interaction. Same-sex couples reported feeling angry, scared, upset, and offended by condemning interactions with extended social network members.

Another type of disconfirmation described by same-sex couples was characterized by extended social network members' avoidance behaviors during interactions regarding marriage amendments. Given that my study specifically focuses on interactions about marriage amendments, the avoidance described here is within interactions rather than a more general avoidance of the couple or communication about the amendments overall. Couples described the ways in which extended social network members avoided acknowledgement of the couples' points of view when discussing marriage amendments. For example, Lynne describes an interaction with a co-worker:

> Lynne: We had work on election day and so we were all talking about it, about voting. Katie walked in to lunch and we were all still talking about it. She sat there for a while and right in the middle of me talking about how important I thought voting against the amendment was she just interrupts and started talking about this report we have due. I mean, I guess she was for it, but she just changed the topic as if I wasn't even talking about something important.

Same-sex couples also described interactions in which extended social network members engaged in avoidance by denying the couple a right to a point of view. For example, Nigella and Giada describe an interaction with a friend of a friend:

> Nigella: We were at this party and the host's friend from work was there. He's been at things before, and I can't stand him. So, the group starts to talk about the amendment passing and generally everyone is mad about it.
> Giada: Yeah, there was this group sense of disappointment except for this guy. He says, well, consider the source. I didn't understand what he meant so I said, what do you mean? Then he says, well, of course you wouldn't know what marriage is really about, would you?
> Nigella: Yeah, I got real annoyed and said, I don't know, something like so you don't think that gay people can have real marriages. Real relationships? And this guy, he basically just rolled his eyes. He left right after.

Although disconfirmation was mentioned by relatively few of the couples I interviewed, disconfirmation is illustrative of a very damaging social consequence of marriage amendments. As previously described by Russell (2000) and Riggle et al. (2009), anti-gay ballot measures lead to GLBT individuals having increased exposure to negative messages about themselves and their relationships. Frost (2011) reports that GLBT individuals perceive their intimacy-related, or relational, pursuits as more devalued than do their heterosexual counterparts in large part due to macrosocial factors, such as laws and policies. The experiences of disconfirmation described by couples I interviewed show how these negative messages can also come on the microsocial level from members of one's social network. Just as extended social network members can add to a positive sense of connection within a community (Blau & Fingerman, 2009), these disconfirming interactions illustrate the ability of extended social network members to have strongly negative influences in our lives. Disconfirming behavior from extended social network members serve to increase negative psychological outcomes for same-sex couples experiencing marriage amendments in their states.

Experiences of Marriage Amendments for GLBT Individuals, Same-sex Couples, and Their Social Networks

Meyer (2003) explains that stress can result not only from personal events, but also from social structures. Minority stress for GLBT people is a chronic psychological strain that results from experiences of being a discriminated-against social minority. Rostosky et al. (2007) found that same-sex couples experience minority stress as they interact with their social network and community and that couples often try to cope with minority stress in a variety of ways. Although same-sex couples develop strategies for coping with minority stress, this stress takes a toll on their relationships (Otis, Rostosky, Riggle, & Hamrin, 2006). Amendments and other laws banning same-sex marriage, and their surrounding debates, have been found to increase minority stress for GLBT people (Riggle, Rostosky, & Horne, 2009; Rostosky et al., 2009). Research by Arm, Horne, and Levitt (2009) and Horne, Rostosky, & Riggle (2011) have shown that the negative psychological effects of marriage amendments and their surrounding de- bates extend to the family members of GLBT people. Thus, the introduc- tion of marriage amendments has negative consequences for GLBT people, same-sex couples, and their social networks.

Yet, research has also shown some positive consequences of the intro- duction of marriage amendments stemming from the fight against and re- sistance to the amendments themselves. As discussed above, GLBT people have reported positive affect, support, greater engagement with political process, a greater political determination, a sense of empowerment, and a strengthening of personal relationships as a result of the struggle against same-sex marriage bans (Maisel & Fingerhut, 2011; Oswald & Kuvlanka, 2008; Riggle et al., 2009; Rostosky et al., 2010). While it would be ridicu- lous to argue that the benefits outweigh the costs of the introduction of marriage amendments for GLBT people, same-sex couples, and their social networks, the relatively positive consequences of the struggle against mar- riage amendments highlight the importance of ties between GLBT people and their social networks, especially in resisting further discrimination.

My study of the interactions between same-sex couples and their ex- tended social network members about marriage amendments shows the powerful role of loose social ties in our experiences of our own identities, relationships, and communities. In my study, social network members both created and mitigated negative consequences of marriage amendments for same-sex couples. Extended social network members served as a source for emotional and material support in same-sex couples' struggles with mar- riage amendments and their consequences. Further, my study demonstrates the reciprocal relationships of social influence among extended social net- works as they suggest that the impact of marriage amendments on same- sex couples may have influenced the thoughts and actions of extended social network members. The influence of same-sex couples' experiences and per- spective on extended social network members was especially evident in in- teractions involving coming out, social support and solidarity. While much of the previous research on interactions among social network members has focused on the influence of social networks on individuals and couples (see Parks, 2007, for overview), much of this previous work limits the level of social network examined to more immediate relationships such as family members and close friends. Taken together, the research on the experiences of marriage amendments emphasizes the importance of considering the bat- tle for and against same-sex marriage as part of a new relational context not just for GLBT people and same-sex couples, but for their close and extended social network members as well

Conclusion

Duringthe time I was writing this book, I had to keep going back to the introduction and revising the number of U.S. states that recognized same-sex marriage, the number of U.S. states that had passed legislation against same-sex marriage, the federal status of U.S. same-sex marriages, and the number of countries that have national recognition for same-sex marriage. It is likely that there will have been more changes to this information by the time you read this book. When I was in graduate school, a wise professor in my department, Dr. John Murphy, was fond of saying, "It's hard to write about a moving target." The legal status of same-sex marriage in the United States is one such "moving target," but it is my hope that this book provides an understanding of the same-sex marriage experiences of U.S. GLBT people, same-sex couples, and their social networks. The research discussed in this book makes it clear that it can be challenging—and joyful—to enact and express relational commitment and manage relationships among social network members in the dynamically changing and new relational context created by same-sex marriage.

The research on same-sex marriage discussed in this book illustrates the utility of approaching the understanding of same-sex marriage from a Communication Studies perspective. Our interactions with one another not only shape our relationships and build our social worlds, but also help to define our identities and sense of self (see Tracy, 2002). Thus, our preceptions of others and ourselves are both influenced by our interactions and influence our interactions. Research presented throughout this book demonstrates how interactions regarding same-sex marriage impacted how GLBT people and their social network members saw themselves, their romantic relationships, their relationships with family and friends, and their view of society in general. For example, couples interactions with their family-of-origin members about same-sex marriage discussed in Chapter 4 demonstrated how these interactions affected couples' views of their place in their families and the indentities of those who had a GLBT relative in a same-sex marriage. As discussed in Chapters 3 and 5, deciding and talking about whether to marry or not affected couples, views of themselvers, their romantic relationships, and their relationship to the GLBT community. The utility of theories of communication, especially relational dialectics theory (Chapter 2; Baxter & Montgomery, 1996) and communication privacy management theory (Chapter 4; Petronio, 2002), to understanding specific experiences of and communication about same-sex marriage is also demonstrated in the research presented in this book.

Our interactions do not occur within a vacuum. Rather, they take place within a multidimensional context that both affects and is affected by our communication. As demonstrated throughout this book, same-sex marriage functions as a new relational context for GLBT people, same-sex couples, and their social networks. Same-sex marriage as a context for communication within relationships is best understood as neither an external force nor product of the relationship, but as both simultaneously. For example, Chapter 2 illustrates the interchange between the introduction of legally recognized same-sex marriage and the ways that GLBT people thought about their romantic relationships, their own desires regarding relationships, their view of the GLBT community, and their understanding of the relationship between the GLBT community and non-GLBT members of society. As discussed in Chapter 3, same-sex marriage is a context which inspired same-sex couples to communicate about whether to marry or not, even if they had been maintaining a committed romantic relationship for a long time without marriage. Chapter 4 demonstrates how communciation and relationships among same-sex couples and their family members affect and are affected by same-sex marriage as a relational context. The same-sex marriage experiences of older same-sex couples discussed in Chapter 5 show the influence of same-sex marriage as part of the changing social context for same-sex relationships in the U.S. over the past half century. Finally, Chapter 6 demonstrates that same-sex marriage is an influential relational context even for GLBT people, same-sex couples, and their social networks who reside in a location that maintains restrictions against legally recognized same-sex marriage.

Limitations of the Research on Same-sex Marriage

The research presented in this book is helpful in understanding the same-sex marriage experiences of GLBT people, same-sex couples and their social networks. Yet, some limitations to this research should be considered. While many of my studies presented in this book share limitations with other research on same-sex marriage, I will discuss the limitations of my research in detail.

First, all of my research studies presented in this book relied on a non-probablity sampling technique known as snowball, or network, sampling.

Snowball sampling techinques are often a productive and efficient way to reach members of minority populations, but like all non-probablity sampling techiques, snowball sampling may be vulnerable to bias resulting from a lack of random sampling (Baxter & Babbie, 2004). When employing the snowball sampling technique, I initially attempted to contact potential participants via announcements through the membership lists of GLBT organizations and list servs. Therefore, participants' responses may not reflect the experiences of those with less GLBT community involvement. The reliance on GLBT listservs for recruitment may have also biased the sample toward those who have the means for and competency with computers, electronic devices, and the internet. In addition, many of the participants in my research studies presented in this book resided in Massachusetts. In part, the reliance on Massachusetts-based GLBT people and same-sex couples was because Massachusetts was the first state to legally recognize same-sex marriage. Yet, the results of some studies may not completely reflect the experiences of same-sex marriage and surrounding debates in other states.

Second, there are some limitations derived from the online survey and IM interview procedures used in most of my research studies that are presented in this book. Again, the reliance on online procedures may have biased my samples toward those who had the means to access and competency with computers, electronic devices, and the internet. The IM interview format was chosen because it allowed for a simultaneous three-way interaction between the couple and the interviewer and alleviated travel and scheduling challenges often associated with face-to-face interviews. The IM interview procedure used was consistent with online interviewing recommendations made by Eedem-Moorefield, Proulx, and Pasley (2008) and James and Busher (2009). Yet, because the interviews were not face-to-face, it is possible the results may differ from those that could be gained from face-to-face interviews where richer nonverbal communication is possible (Hinchcliffe & Gavin, 2009).

Further, many of my research studies presented in this book relied on interviews conducted with both members of a same-sex couple simultaniously. Interviewing both members of the couple simultaniously may have lead to more inclusive data about the couples' experiences than would interviewing only one partner as is common in much marriage research (Matthews, 2005). However, simultaneously interviewing the couple may have led participants to respond differently to questions than they may have if interviewed separately. There is no way to know if participants may have shaped their responses to be more acceptable to their partners due to the interview procedure. Further, the studies describe interactions with social network members from the perspective of the

GLBT participants only. It is possible that firsthand accounts of the interactions from the social network members may differ from the descriptions provided by the participants.

Future Directions and Concluding Thoughts

Legally recognized same-sex marriage in the United States is still relatively new, regionally limited, and under fire. As the institution of same-sex marriage spreads, matures, and continues to be challenged in the United States, the experiences of GLBT people, same-sex couples, and their social networks will continue to affect and be affected by same-sex marriage as a new relational context. Future studies should continue to examine experiences of same-sex marriage.

Two types of future research on same-sex marriage experiences are especially needed. First, as discussed in Chapter 5, studies need to include more diverse samples of GLBT people, same-sex couples, and their social network members so that the range of same-sex marriage experiences may be better understood. Future studies should continue to consider the intersection of multiple minority social identities to better understand the same-sex marriage experiences of a variety of members of the GLBT community (McCall, 2005). The racial and ethnic diversity of samples in studies of same-sex marriage experiences should be expanded. Further, there is a need for more studies of the same-sex marriage experiences of transgender individuals, their partners, and social network members.

Second, future research should examine the same-sex marriage experiences of GLBT people, same-sex couples, and their social networks as same-sex marriage matures. Most of the studies discussed in this book examine the introduction of same-sex marriage and its impact. Therefore, most of the same-sex couples included as participants in the studies detailed in this book had formed and maintained their committed relationship before marriage was a legal option. Yet, same-sex marriage has been available to couples in Massachusetts for nearly a decade. Thus, many same-sex couples in the United States will now initiate their romantic relationships with legal marriage as an available option. Future studies should investigate the same-sex marriage experiences of couples who initiated their relationships with marriage as an option as compared to same-sex couples who initiated their relationships without legal marriage as an option. While the future of same-sex marriage in the United States is still uncertain, a June 2013 poll indicated that most Americans surveyed believed that legally recognized same-sex marriage in the United States was inevitable (PEW Research Center, 2013). It is likely that future generations of GLBT people will come of age and enact all of their relationships in an environment in which legal marriage for American same-sex couples is possible. Future research should examine the

same-sex marriage experiences of these GLBT people who did not experience a time when marriage was not possible.

Same-sex marriage forms a dynamic, complex, and multidimensional
context for the relationships of American GLBT people, same-sex couples,
and their social networks. There is a reciprocal relationship between context and the communication we have with one another. This communication
is also interdependent with our understanding of ourselves and our relationships. The perceptions, communication, and relationships of American
GLBT people, same-sex couples, and their social networks will continue to
affect and be affected by the availability of same-sex marriage in some
states, the moves to ban same-sex marriage in other states, and the national
debate about same-sex marriage. Future research should continue to focus
on the experiences of GLBT people, same-sex couples, and their social networks within the context of same-sex marriage.

Notes

Chapter Two

1   Participants were recruited through a snowball sampling method and were asked to complete an online survey. In this recruitment method, messages about the study were sent to the listservs and message boards of GLBT organizations. Those who completed the study were then asked to pass information about the study on to others who fit the participation criteria. Eeden-Moorefield, Proulx, and Pasley (2008) and Riggle, Rostosky, and Reedy (2005) point out that internet-based participant recruitment may benefit GLBT research by giving researchers wider access to more diverse perspectives within the GLBT community in a more efficient way than other recruitment sites such as GLBT community centers.

2   Two-hundred eighty-eight people participated in the study; 169 participants were female, 113 were male, and 6 identified as neither male nor female. Participant ages ranged from 19 to 66 years old ($M = 31.6$, $Mdn = 30$, $SD = 9.6$) Most participants were Caucasian ($N = 262$), 15 participants were African American, 3 were Asian, and 8 did not identify a racial or ethnic heritage. Participants identified themselves as gay or lesbian ($N = 235$), bisexual ($N = 44$) and queer/transgendered ($N = 9$), and had identified themselves as such for an average of 11.4 years ($Mdn = 10$, $SD = 7.89$). Most participants described themselves as "totally" ($N = 161$) or "mostly" ($N = 114$) out about their sexual orientation, while the rest ($N = 13$) indicated that they were out to only a few people. One-hundred ninety-three participants were currently involved in a primary romantic relationship, and the length of those relationships ranged from 1 to 36 years ($M = 5.50$, $Mdn = 4$, $SD = 4.80$). Data analysis used an inductive approach and a constant comparative method (see Chapter 3, Note 2; Strauss & Corbin, 2008). For more details, please see Lannutti (2005, 2007a).

Chapter Three

1   Participants were recruited through a snowball sampling method similar to that described in Chapter 2, Note 1, and were asked to complete an online survey. Two-hundred sixty-three people participated in the study. Sixty-five percent of the participants were female, 33% were male, and 2% identified as neither male nor female. Seventy-seven percent of participants identified as either gay or lesbian, 20% identified as bisexual, and 3% identified as queer. Participant ages ranged from 23 to 54 ($M = 34.46$, $Mdn = 32$, $SD = 7.87$). Most participants were Caucasian (88%), 5% were Hispanic, 2%

were African American, and 2% were Asian, and 3% did not provide racial/ethnic information. All participants were currently involved in a same-sex relationship, and the average relationship length was 7.45 years (Mdn = 6, SD = 5.11). Seventy-two percent of the participants were legally married to their partner, and all had gotten married within the previous 13 months since Massachusetts began issuing marriage licenses to same-sex couples. The remaining participants (28%) were engaged to be married to their partner within the next 16 months. A subsection of the participants (15%), all of whom were currently legally married, had a commitment ceremony with their partner before same-sex marriage was legally recognized. Data analysis used an inductive approach and a constant comparative method (see Chapter 3, Note 2; Strauss & Corbin, 2008). For more details, please see Lannutti (2008).

2   Thirty-seven same-sex couples living in Massachusetts (which had recognized same-sex marriage at the time) but were not married or engaged were interviewed. Couples were recruited using a snowball sampling method similar to that described in Chapter 2, Note 1. Twenty of the couples were female-female, and 17 were male-male couples. All participants identified as gay or lesbian. All couples cohabitated. Ages ranged from 25 to 50 (M = 36.39, Mdn = 35.50, SD = 6.40). Relationship length ranged from 3 to 24 years (M = 8.14, Mdn = 7, SD = 4.69). Most participants identified as Caucasian (71.6%, N = 53), while other participants identified as African American (N = 11), Hispanic (N = 5), and Asian (N = 5). Four of the couples were interracial couples. Recruitment took place in two phases. First, a sample of 20 couples was recruited and interviewed. The second phase of participant recruitment took place after the 20 initial interviews were analyzed. The goal of the second phase of participant recruitment and interviewing was to ensure that the emerging data analysis categories were saturated. Saturation occurs when new data do not lead to new theoretical insights about categories or the relationship between categories (Charmaz, 2006; Strauss & Corbin, 2008). The recruitment criteria and procedures for the additional sample were the same as that for the initial sample. Saturation was reached after 17 additional couples were interviewed. The data from the initial set of interviews were analyzed using an inductive method (Charmaz, 2000). When using this type of data-driven approach, themes emerge from the participants' responses rather than a priori conceptual categories or themes (Boyatzis, 1998). Using procedures recommended by Strauss and Corbin (2008), the first step in analyzing the initial interviews was open coding. Open coding was performed for each of the participants' responses to questions or each other's statements during the interview to identify key concepts in the data. Consistent with Strauss and Corbin (2008), the relationships among concepts in the data were analyzed to form themes. Participants' responses in the second set of interviews were analyzed using comparative analysis (Strauss & Corbin, 2008). In this process, concepts that are similar to those already included in identified themes from the initial sample remain included in those existing themes while concepts that are not consistent with existing themes are used to form new themes. After all concepts from the second set of interviews were coded into themes, concepts from the initial sample were comparatively analyzed to see if they fit better with those first generated from the second set of interviews. Thus, all of the concepts from the entire data set were compared to all themes and placed into themes representative of the entire data set. Once all of the themes derived from the inductive comparative analysis process were established, theoretical linkages among themes were examined. Notes were taken throughout the coding process to identify exemplar quotations for the themes. Steps were taken to check the trustworthiness of the data analysis (Lincoln & Guba, 1985; Miles & Huberman, 1994). Member checks were conducted

with some participating couples who reviewed themes and exemplars that emerged from data analysis and confirmed that the descriptions fit with their experiences.

3   Interviews were conducted using instant messenger (IM) with the following procedure: The recruitment announcement instructed those who were interested in the study to contact the researcher by email. When emails from potential participants were received, the researcher responded by sending a consent form with details about the study to the potential participant and indicated that in order to participate each member of the couple would need to send informed consent back to the researcher in separate emails. After informed consent was received from both members of the couple, an interview time was scheduled. Interviews took place using the chat function of a popular instant messenger (IM) program that was available for free to all participants. This interview format was chosen because it allowed for a simultaneous three-way interaction between the couple and the interviewer and alleviated travel and scheduling challenges often associated with face-to-face interviews. The IM interview procedure is consistent with online interviewing recommendations made by Eedem-Moorefield, Proulx, and Pasley (2008) and James and Busher (2009). To protect the participants' confidentiality, they were asked to create a new IM screen name to be used exclusively for the purposes of the interview. Interviews were semi-standardized such that an interview protocol with some predetermined questions was used for all interviews, but each interview ultimately developed in reaction to participants' responses (Berg, 1995). Interviews lasted between 45 and 75 minutes. Quotes from IM interviews may have been edited to reflect standard English grammar and spelling, such as replacing "u" with "you."

Chapter Four

1   Participants were recruited through a snowball sampling method similar to that described in Chapter 2, Note 1. Forty-eight couples (27 female-female, 21 male-male) were interviewed. Participants lived in 15 Massachusetts towns. All participants identified as gay or lesbian. Participant ages ranged from 23 to 58 years ($M = 35.41$, $Mdn = 33$, $SD = 8.54$). Most participants identified as Caucasian (74 %, $N = 71$), while others identified as African American ($N = 12$), Hispanic ($N = 8$), and Asian ($N = 5$). Six were interracial couples. Most couples ($N = 44$) were married, while 4 couples were engaged and planning to marry during the 5 months following the interview. The current length relationships ranged from 2 to 23 years ($M = 7.25$, $Mdn = 6$, $SD = 4.33$). Nine couples (8 female-female; 1 male-male) had children. Participant recruitment and data analysis procedures were similar to that described in Chapter 3, Note 2. For more details, please see Lannutti (2013).

2   The forty-eight couples participated in IM interviews using a procedure described in Chapter 3, Note 3. Interviews lasted between 45 and 75 minutes. All interviews began with questions about participants' demographic information and background information about their relationship. The majority of the interview time was spent discussing the interactions the couples had with members of their families about their decision to marry and marriage.

Chapter Five

1   Female-female couples in which one partner identified as bisexual and the other identified as lesbian were sought for this study. Twenty-six bisexual-lesbian couples were interviewed. All participants were residents of Massachusetts and lived in 15 towns within the state. Most participants were Caucasian ($N = 37$) while six were Asian, five

were African American, and four were Hispanic. Participant ages ranged from 24 to 57 years ($M = 35.71$, $Mdn = 34$, $SD = 8.54$). All participants lived full-time with their partner and had an exclusive relationship. The average age difference between partners was 2.73 years ($Mdn = 1.5$, $SD = 3.44$). The majority of the couples (85%, $N = 22$) had married since Massachusetts started legally recognizing same-sex marriages in May 2004. The remaining four couples were engaged to be married and were planning weddings during the 8 months following the interviews. The length of time that participants had been in their relationships ranged from 2.5 to 15 years ($M = 6.42$, $Mdn = 5.75$, $SD = 3.21$). Six of the couples had a commitment ceremony prior to the legal recognition of same-sex marriage in Massachusetts. None of the participants had a marriage or commitment ceremony with a previous same-sex partner, but three of the bisexual participants had been previously married to a man. Five of the couples were interracial couples. Four of the couples were currently raising children together. The couples participated in IM interviews using a procedure described in Chapter 3, Note 3. Interviews lasted between 45 and 90 minutes. All interviews began with questions about participants' demographic information and background information about their relationship. The majority of the interview time was spent discussing the ways in which the couples' marriage and/or decision to marry impacted their romantic relationship and their relationships with others. Participant recruitment and data analysis procedures were similar to those described in Chapter 3, Note 2. See Lannutti (2007b) for more details about the study.

2   Using a snowball sampling method similar to that describe in Chapter 2, Note 1, same-sex couples with both members over 50 who had been together for at least one year and resided in Massachusetts were sought for the study. Thirty-six same-sex couples (20 female-female, 16 male-male) were interviewed. Twenty-two couples (12 female-female, 10 male-male) had been legally married since Massachusetts began recognizing same-sex marriage in 2004 and 14 (8 female-female couples, 6 male-male couples) were not legally married or engaged. All of the couples resided together full time in one of 13 Massachusetts cities or towns. No couple had children under 18 living in the home. All male participants identified as gay and all female participants identified as lesbian. Participants had identified as gay or lesbian for an average of 38.21 years ($Mdn = 40$, $SD = 7.77$). Participants' ages ranged from 56 to 73 ($M = 63.75$, $Mdn = 63$, $SD = 3.86$). The average age difference between partners was two years ($Mdn = 1$, $SD = 2.43$). Relationship length ranged from 7 to 43 years ($M = 18.44$, $Mdn = 15$, $SD = 9.13$). Marital status did not significantly differ as a function of participant age ($t(34) = 1.07$, $p = .29$) or relationship length ($t(34) = .61$, $p = .55$). Most of the couples consisted of two Caucasian individuals ($N = 29$), three consisted of two African American individuals, and four consisted of two individuals with differing racial/ethnic backgrounds. Because participants were located across Massachusetts, face-to-face interviews were not possible. Participants were asked to indicate whether they preferred a telephone interview or an IM interview. The interview formats both allowed for a simultaneous three-way interaction between the couple and the interviewer. Twenty-four couples preferred phone interviews while 12 preferred an IM interview. Interviews were semi-standardized such that an interview guide with some predetermined questions and topics was used for all interviews, but each interview ultimately developed in reaction to participants' responses (Berg, 1995). IM interviews followed a procedure similar to that described in Chapter 3, Note 3. All interviews began with questions about participants' demographic information and background information about their relationship. Next, participants were asked about their reactions to legally recognized same-sex marriage and the surrounding debates, how legally recognized same-sex marriage has impacted their relationship

with one another and their social networks, and about their own decisions to marry or not. Interviews lasted between 45 and 75 minutes. Participant recruitment and data analysis procedures were similar to that described in Chapter 3, Note 2. See Lannutti (2011a) for more details about the study.

Chapter Six

1   Between six and twelve months after the November 2006 ratification of marriage amendments in various U.S. States, same-sex couples residing in seven U.S. States with new marriage amendments were recruited and interviewed regarding their experiences regarding the marriage amendments. Participant recruitment and data analysis procedures were similar to that reported in Chapter 2, Note 1 and Chapter 3, Note 2. The study used an IM interview procedure similar to that described in Chapter 3, Note 3. All interviews began with questions about participants' demographic information and background information about their relationship and proceeded to questions about their experiences regarding the marriage amendments. Interviews lasted between 45 and 60 minutes. Interviews focused on interactions regarding the marriage amendments among the couple and their extended social network members. More specifically, this study reports on participants' responses to questions about their social interactions regarding the marriage amendments with people who are part of their social network, such as work colleagues, team members, and casual friends, but are not considered to be close friends or family members by either member of the couple. Some extended social network members had contact with both members of the couple, while others were in contact with only one member of the couple. See Lannutti (2011b) for more information about the study.

2   A total of 57 couples (32 female-female couples and 25 male-male couples) were interviewed. The couples resided in one of seven U.S. States that had passed marriage amendments during the 2006 elections: 8 in Alabama, 12 in South Carolina, 14 in Virginia, 7 in Wisconsin, 2 in South Dakota, 9 in Tennessee, and 5 in Idaho. The couples had been together in their romantic relationship for between 1 and 14 years ($M = 6.04$, $Mdn = 6$, $SD = 3.40$). Participant ages ranged from 23 to 60 years ($M = 37.80$, $Mdn = 37.5$, $SD = 8.67$). Most couples included two Caucasian individuals (78%), while others included individuals that were both African-American (5%), both Asian-American (4%), both Hispanic-American (3%), or two individuals with differing ethnic backgrounds (10%). See Lannutti (2011b) for more information about the study.

References

Alderson, K. & Lahey, K. A. (2004). *Same-sex marriage: The personal and the political.* New York: Insomniac Press.

Allport, G. W. (1954). *The nature of prejudice.* Reading, MA: Addison-Wesley.

Amato, P.R. (2012). The well-being of children with gay and lesbian parents. *Social Science Research, 41,* 771–774.

American Psychological Association. (2005). *Lesbian and Gay Parenting* http://www.apa.org/pi/lgbt/resources/parenting-full.pdf. Accessed August 7, 2013.

Argyle, M. & Henderson, M. (1984). The rules of friendship. *Journal of Social and Personal Relationships, 1,* 211–237.

Arm, J. R., Horne, S. G., & Levitt, H. M. (2009). Negotiating connection to GLBT experience: Family members' experience of anti-GLBT movements and policies. *Journal of Counseling Psychology, 56,* 82–96.

Attridge, M. (1994). Barriers to the dissolution of romantic relationships. In D. J. Canary & L. Stafford, *Communication and relational maintenance.* (pp. 141–164). San Diego, CA: Academic Press.

Badgett, M.V.L. (2009). *When gay people get married: What happens when societies legalize same-sex marriage.* New York: NYU Press.

Bar, H. & Eady, E. (1998). The role of intergroup contact in change of prejudice and ethnic relations. In P. Katz,(Ed.), *Toward the elimination of racism.* (pp. 245–308). New York: Pergamon.

Barker, J. C., Herdt, G., & de Vries, B. (2006). Social support in the lives of lesbians and gay men at midlife and later. *Sexuality Research & Social Policy, 3,* 1–23.

Baxter, L. A. (2011). *Voicing relationships: A dialogic perspective.* Thousand Oaks, CA: SAGE.

Baxter, L. A., & Babbie, E. (2004). *The basics of communication research.* Belmont, CA: Wadsworth/Thomson.

Baxter, L. A., Dun, T., & Sahlstein, E. (2001). Rules for relating communicated among social network members. *Journal of Social and Personal Relationships, 18,* 173–199.

Baxter, L. A., Henauw, C., Huisman, D., Livesay, C. B., Norwood, K., Su, H., Wolf, B., & Young, B. (2009). Lay conceptions of "family": A replication and extension. *Journal of Family Communication, 9,* 179–189.

Baxter, L. A. & Montgomery, B. M. (1996). *Relating: Dialogues and dialectics.* New York: Guilford Press.

Beeler, J. & DiProva, V. (1999). Family adjustment following disclosure of homosexuality by a member: Themes discerned in narrative accounts. *Journal of Marital and Family Therapy, 25,* 443–459.

Berg, B. L. (1995). *Qualitative research methods for the social sciences, 2nd Ed.* Boston, MA: Allyn and Bacon.

Berger, R. M. & Kelly, J. J. (1996). Gay men and lesbians grown older. In R. P. Cabaj & T. S. Stein (Eds.), *Textbook of homosexuality and mental health*. Washington, DC: American Psychiatric Press.

Blau, M. & Fingerman, K. L. (2009). *Consequential strangers: The power of people who don't seem to matter...but really do*. New York: W.W. Norton & Company.

Blevins, D. & Werth, Jr., J. L. (2006). End-of-life issues for LGBT older adults. In D. Kimmel, T. Rose, & S. David (Eds.), *Lesbian, gay, bisexual, and transgendered aging: Research and clinical perspectives*. (pp. 206–226). New York: Columbia University Press.

Boyatzis, R. E. (1998). *Transforming qualitative information: Thematic analysis and code development*. Thousand Oaks, CA: SAGE.

Brown, R. (1995). *Prejudice: Its social psychology*. Oxford, UK: Blackwell.

Burleson, W. E. (2005). *Bi America: Myths, truths, and struggles of an invisible community*. Binghamton, New York: Harrington Park Press.

Caron, S. L. & Ulin, M. (1997). Closeting and the quality of lesbian relationships. *Families in Society: The Journal of Contemporary Human Services, 78*, 413–419.

Caughlin, J. P. & Petronio, S. (2004). Privacy in families. In Vangelisti, A. L.(Ed.), *Handbook of family communication*. (pp. 379–412). Mahwah, NJ: LEA.

Charmaz, K. (2000). Grounded theory: Objectivist and constructivist methods. In N. K. Denzin & Y. S. Lincoln (Eds.), *Handbook of qualitative research*. (pp. 509–535). Thousand Oaks, CA: SAGE.

Charmaz, K. (2006). *Constructing grounded theory: A practical guide through qualitative analysis*. Thousand Oaks, CA: SAGE.

Child, J. T., Petronio, S., Agyeman-Buda, E. A., & Westermann, D. A. (2011). Blog scrubbing: Exploring triggers that change privacy rules. *Computers in Human Behavior, 27*, 2017–2027.

Christakis, N. A. & Fowler, J. H. (2009). *Connected: The surprising power of our social networks and how they shape our lives*. New York: Little, Brown and Company.

Cook-Daniels, L. (2008). Living memory GLBT history timeline: Current elders would have been this old when these events happened....*Journal of GLBT Family Studies, 4*, 485–497.

Crosbie-Burnett, M., Foster, T. L., Murray, C. I., & Bowen, G. I. (1996). Gays' and lesbians' families-of-origin: A social-cognitive-behavioral model of adjustment. *Family Relations, 45*, 397–403.

Cunningham, M. & Barbee, A. (2000). Social support. In C. Hendricks & S. S. Hendricks (Eds.), *Close relationships: A sourcebook*. (pp. 273–285). Thousand Oaks, CA: SAGE.

D'Augelli, A. R. (2005). Stress and adaptation among families of lesbian, gay, and bisexual youth: Research challenges. *Journal of GLBT Family Studies, 1*, 115–134.

Dindia, K. (2000). Relational maintenance. In C. Hendrick & S. S. Hendrick,(Eds.), *Close relationships: A sourcebook*. (pp. 287–300). Thousand Oaks, CA: SAGE.

Dindia, K. (2003). Definitions and perspectives on relational maintenance communication. In D. J. Canary & M. Dainton (Eds.), *Maintaining relationships through communication*. (pp. 1–30). Mahwah, NJ: LEA.

DiPlacido, J. (1998). Minority stress among lesbians, gay men, and bisexuals: A consequent of heterosexism, homophobia, and stigmatization. In G. M. Herek (Ed.), *Stigma and sexual orientation: Understanding prejudice against lesbians, gay men, and bisexuals*. (pp. 138–159) Thousand Oaks, CA: SAGE.

Eedem-Moorefield, B., Proulx, C. M., and Pasley, K. (2008). A comparison of internet and face-to-face (FTF) qualitative methods in studying the relationships of gay men. *Journal of GLBT Family Studies, 4*, 181–204.

Eggebeen, D. J. (2012). What can we learn from studies of children raised by gay or lesbian parents? *Social Science Research, 41*, 775–778.

Elder, G. H. (1994). Time, human agency, and social change: Perspectives on the life course. *Social Psychology Quarterly, 57*, 4–15.

Ellison, C. G., Acevedo, G. A., & Ramos-Wada, A. I. (2011). Religion and attitudes toward same-sex marriage among U.S. Latinos. *Social Science Quarterly, 92*, 35–56.

Frost, D. M. (2011). Similarities and differences in the pursuit of intimacy among sexual minority and heterosexual individuals: A personal projects analysis. *Journal of Social Issues, 67*, 282–301.

Gabbay, S. G. & Wahler, J. J. (2002). Lesbian aging: Review of a growing literature. *Journal of Gay and Lesbian Social Services, 14*, 1–21.

Galupo, M. P. & Pearl, M. L. (2007). Bisexual attitudes toward same-sex marriage. *Journal of Bisexuality, 7*, 287–301.

Ghavanmi, N. & Johnson, K. L. (2011). Comparing sexual and ethnic minority perspectives on same-sex marriage. *Journal of Social Issues, 67*, 394–412.

Goldberg, A. E. (2010). *Lesbian and gay parents and their children.* Washington, DC: American Psychological Association.

Goldberg, A. E. & Kuvlanka, K. A. (2012). Marriage (in)equality: The perspectives of adolescents and emerging adults with lesbian, gay, and bisexual parents. *Journal of Marriage and Family, 74*, 34–52.

Goodridge v. Department of Public Health. SJC-08860, November 18, 2003.

Gottman, J. M., Levenson, R. W., Gross, J., Frederickson, B. L., McCoy, K., Rosenthal, L., Ruef, A., & Yoshimoto, D. (2003). Correlates of gay and lesbian couples' relationship satisfaction and relationship dissolution. *Journal of Homosexuality, 45*, 23–43.

Grossman, A. H. (2006). Physical and mental health of older lesbian, gay, and bisexual adults. In D. Kimmel, T. Rose, & S. David (Eds.), *Lesbian, gay, bisexual, and transgendered aging: Research and clinical perspectives.* (pp. 53–69). New York: Columbia University Press.

Haas, S. M. & Stafford, L. (1998). An initial examination of maintenance behaviors in gay and lesbian relationships. *Journal of Social and Personal Relationships, 15*, 846–855.

Haas, S. M. & Stafford, L. (2005). Maintenance behaviors in same-sex and marital relationships: A matched sample comparison. *Journal of Family Communication, 5*, 43–60.

Halderman, D. C. (1998). Ceremonies and religion in same-sex marriage. In R. J. Cabaj & D. W. Purcell (Eds.), *On the road to same-sex marriage: A supportive guide to psychological, political and legal issues.* (pp. 165–190). San Francisco: Jossey-Bass Inc.

Hall, G. (2005). "These are my parents": The experiences of children in same-sex parented families during the first year of marriage legalization in Massachusetts. In *What I did for love, or benefits, or...: Same-sex marriage in Massachusetts. Wellesley Centers for Women, Working Paper No. 422.* (pp. 35–45). Wellesley, MA: Wellesley Centers for Women.

Herek, G. M. (Ed.) (1998). *Stigma and sexual orientation: Understanding prejudice against lesbians, gay men, and bisexuals.* Thousand Oaks, CA: SAGE.

Hinchcliffe, V. & Gavin, H. (2009). Social and virtual networks: Evaluating synchronous online interviewing using instant messenger. *The Qualitative Report, 14*, 318–340.

Holt, M. (2011). Gay men and ambivalence about "gay community:" From gay community attachment to personal communities. *Culture, Health, & Sexuality, 13*, 857–871.

Horne, S. G., Rostosky, S. S., & Riggle, E. D. B. (2011). Marriage restriction amendments and family members of lesbian, gay, bisexual individuals: A mixed-method approach. *Journal of Social Issues, 67*, 358–375.

Human Rights Campaign (n.d.), *Marriage.* Retrieved June 3, 2013 from http://www.hrc.org/issues/marriage.asp.

Hunter, S. (2005). *Midlife and older LGBT adults: Knowledge and affirmative practice for the social services.* New York: Haworth Press.

Hunter, S. (2007). *Coming out and disclosures: LGBT persons across the lifespan.* New York: Haworth Press.

Hutchins, L. (1996). Bisexuality: Politics and community. In B. Firestein (Ed.), *Bisexuality: The psychology and politics of an invisible minority.* (pp. 240—259). Thousand Oaks, CA: SAGE.

Iasenza, S., Colucci, P. L., & Rothberg, B. (1996). Coming out and the mother-daughter bond: Two case examples. In J. Laird & R. Green.(Eds.), *Lesbians and gays in couples and families: A handbook for therapists.* (pp. 123—136). San Francisco: Jossey-Bass Publishers.

Israel, T. & Mohr, J. J. (2004). Attitudes toward bisexual woman and men: Current research, future directions. In R. C. Fox (Ed.), *Current research on bisexuality.* (pp. 117—134). Binghamton, NY: Harrington Park Press.

James, N. & Busher, H. (2009). *Online interviewing.* Thousand Oaks, CA: SAGE.

Jay, K. (1999). *Tales of the lavender menace: A memoir of liberation.* New York: Basic Books.

Johnson, M. P. (1982). Social and cognitive features of the dissolution of commitment to relationships. In S. Duck (Ed.), *Personal relationships 4: Dissolving personal relationships.* (pp. 51—74). London: Academic Press.

Johnson, M. P. (1991). Commitment to personal relationships. In W. H. Jones & D. Perlman (Eds.), *Advances in personal relationships, Vol 3.* (pp. 117—143.) London: Kingsley.

Khan, F. A. (2011). Powerful cultural productions: Identity politics in diasporic same-sex South Asian weddings. *Sexualities, 14,* 377—398.

Kimmel, D., Rose, T., Orel, N. & Greene. B. (2006). Historical context for research on lesbian, gay, bisexual and transgendered aging. In D. Kimmel, T. Rose, & S. David(Eds.), *Lesbian, gay, bisexual, and transgendered aging: Research and clinical perspectives.* (pp. 1—19). New York: Columbia University Press.

Knee, C. R., Nanayakkara, A., Vieter, N. A., Neighbors, C., & Patrick, H. (2001). Implicit theories of relationships: Who cares if romantic partners are less than ideal? *Personality and Social Psychology Bulletin, 27,* 808—819.

Knee, C. R., Patrick, H., & Lonsbary, C. (2003). Implicit theories of relationships: Orientations toward evaluation and cultivation. *Personality and Social Psychology Review, 7,* 41—55.

Koening Kellas, J. & Suter, E. A. (2012). Accounting for lesbian-headed families: Lesbian mothers' responses to discursive challenges. *Communication Monographs, 79,* 475—498.

Kurdek, L. A. (1991). Sexuality in homosexual and heterosexual couples. In K. McKinney and S. Sprecher (Eds.), *Sexuality in close relationships.* (pp. 177—191). Hillsdale, NJ: LEA.

Kurdek, L. A. (2000). Attractions and constraints as determinants of relationship commitment: Longitudinal evidence from gay, lesbian, and heterosexual couples. *Personal Relationships, 7,* 245—262.

Kurdek, L. A. (2004). Are gay and lesbian cohabiting couples really different from heterosexual married couples? *Journal of Marriage and the Family, 66,* 880—900.

Kurdek, L. A. & Schmitt, J. P. (1987). Perceived emotional support from family and friends in members of homosexual, married, and heterosexual cohabiting couples. *Journal of Homosexuality, 14,* 57—68.

Lannutti, P. J. (2005). For better or worse: Exploring the meanings of same-sex marriage within the lesbian, gay, bisexual and transgendered community. *Journal of Social and Personal Relationships, 22,* 5—18.

Lannutti, P. J. (2007a). The influence of same-sex marriage on the understanding of same-sex relationships. *Journal of Homosexuality, 53,* 135—151.

Lannutti, P. J. (2007b). "This is not a lesbian wedding": Examining same-sex marriage and bisexual-lesbian couples. *Journal of Bisexuality, 3–4,* 239–260.

Lannutti, P. J. (2008). Attractions and obstacles while considering legally recognized same-sex marriage. *Journal of GLBT Family Studies, 4,* 245–264.

Lannutti, P. J. (2011a). Security, recognition, and misgivings: Exploring older same-sex couples' experiences of legally recognized same-sex marriage. *Journal of Social and Personal Relationships, 28,* 64–82.

Lannutti, P. J. (2011b). Examining communication about marriage amendments: Same-sex couples and their extended social networks. *Journal of Social Issues, 67,* 264–281.

Lannutti, P. J. (2013). Same-sex marriage and privacy management: Examining couples' communication with family members. *Journal of Family Communication, 13,* 60–75.

LaSala, M. C. (2001). Monogamous or not: Understanding and counseling gay male couples. *Families in Society, 82,* 605–611.

Levitt, H. M., Overebo, E., Anderson-Cleveland, M.B., Loene, C., Jeong, J. Y., Arm, J. R. Horne, S.G. (2009). Balancing dangers: GLBT experience in a time of anti-GLBT legislation. *Journal of Counseling Psychology, 56,* 67–81.

Lincoln, Y. S. & Guba, E. G. (1985). *Naturalistic inquiry.* Beverly Hills, CA: SAGE.

Macintosh, H., Reissuing, E. D., & Andruff, H. (2010). Same-sex marriage in Canada: The impact of legal marriage on the first cohort of gay and lesbian Canadians to wed. *The Canadian Journal of Human Sexuality, 19,* 79–90.

Maisel, N. C. & Fingerhut, A. W. (2011). California's ban on same-sex marriage: The campaign and its effects on gay, lesbian, and bisexual individuals. *Journal of Social Issues, 67,* 242–263.

Marcus, E. (2002). *Making gay history: The half-century fight for lesbian and gay equal rights.* New York: Perennial.

Marks, L. (2012). Same-sex parenting and children's outcomes: A closer examination of the American psychological associations' brief on lesbian and gay parenting. *Social Science Research, 41,* 735–751.

Matthews, S. H. (2005). Crafting qualitative research articles on marriages and families. *Journal of Marriage and the Family, 67,* 799–808.

McCall, L. (2005). The complexity of intersectionality. *Journal of Women in Culture and Society, 30,* 1771–1800.

McGinnis, S. L. (2003). Cohabitating, dating, and perceived costs of marriage: A model of marriage entry. *Journal of Marriage and Family, 65,* 105–116.

McQueeney, K. B. (2003). The new religious rite: A symbolic interactionist case study of lesbian commitment rituals. *Journal of Lesbian Studies, 7,* 49–70.

Meyer, I. H. (2003). Prejudice, social stress, and mental health in lesbian, gay, and bisexual populations: Conceptual issues and research evidence. *Psychological Bulletin, 129,* 674–707.

Meyer, J. (1990). Guess who's coming to dinner this time? A study of gay intimate relationships and the support of those relationships. *Journal of Homosexuality, 16,* 59–82.

Mikcki-Enyart, S. L. (2011). Parent-in-law privacy management: An examination of the links among relational uncertainty, topic avoidance, in-group status, and in-law satisfaction. *Journal of Family Communication, 11,* 237–263.

Miles, M. B. & Huberman, A. M. (1994). *Qualitative data analysis: An expanded sourcebook.* Thousand Oaks, CA: SAGE.

Moore, M. R. (2011). *Invisible families: Gay identities, relationship, and motherhood among Black women.* Berkeley, CA: University of California Press.

Mulick, P. S. & Wright, L. W. (2002). Examining the existence of biphobia in the heterosexual and homosexual populations. *Journal of Bisexuality, 2,* 45–64.

Nagoshi, J. L., Brzuzy, S., & Terrell, H. K. (2012). Deconstructing the complex perceptions of gender roles, gender identity, and sexual orientation among transgender individuals. *Feminism & Psychology, 22,* 405–422.

Norwood, K. (2012a). Transitioning meanings? Family members' communicative struggles surrounding transgender identity. *Journal of Family Communication, 12,* 75–92.

Norwood, K. (2012b). Grieving gender: Trans-identities, transition, and ambiguous loss. *Communication Monographs, 80,* 24–45.

Ochs, R. (1996). Biphobia: It goes more than two ways. In B. Firestein (Ed.), *Bisexuality: The psychology and politics of an invisible minority.* (pp. 217–239). Thousand Oaks, CA: SAGE.

Oppenheimer, V. (2000). The continuing importance of men's economic position in marriage formation. In L. J. Waite (Ed.), *The ties that bind: Perspectives on marriage and cohabitation.* pp. 283–301). New York: Aldine deGruyter.

Osborne, C. (2012). Further comments on the papers by Marks and Regnerus. *Social Science Research, 41,* 799–783.

Oswald, R. F, Blume, L. B, & Marks, S. R. (2005). Decentering heteronormativity: A model for family studies. In V. Bengstron, A. Acock, K. Allen, P. Dilworth-Anderson, & D. Klein (Eds.), *Sourcebook of family theory and research.* (pp. 143–154). Thousand Oaks, CA; SAGE.

Oswald, R. F. & Kuvlanka, K. A. (2008). Same-sex couples legal complexities. *Journal of Family Issues, 29,* 1051–1066.

Otis, M. D., Rostosky, S. S., Riggle, E. D. B., & Hamrin, R. (2006). Stress and relationship quality in same-sex couples. *Journal of Social and Personal Relationships, 23,* 81–99.

Parks, M. R. (2007). *Personal relationships and personal networks.* Mahwah, NJ: LEA.

Parks, M. R. & Eggert, L. L. (1991). The role of context in the dynamics of personal relationships. In W. H. Jones & D. Perlman (Eds.), *Advances in personal relationships.* (pp. 1–34). London: Jessica Kingsley Publishers.

Patterson, D. G., Ciabattari, T., & Schwartz, P. (1999). The constraints of innovation: Commitment and stability among same-sex couples. In J. M. Adams & W. H. Jones (Eds.), *Handbook of interpersonal commitment and relationship stability: Perspectives on individual differences.* (pp. 339–359). Dordrecht, Netherlands: Kluwer Academic Publishers.

Patterson, D. G. & Schwartz, P. (1994). The social construction of conflict in intimate relationships. In D. D. Cahn (Ed.), *Conflict in personal relationships.* Hillsdale, NJ: Erlbaum.

Perrin, E. C., Siegel, B. S., & the Committee on the Psychological Aspects of Child and Family Health. (2013). Promoting the well-being of children whose parents are gay or lesbian. *Pediatrics, 131,* e1374–e1383. DOI: i0.1542/peds.2013–0377.

Petronio, S. (2002). *Boundaries of privacy: Dialectics of disclosure.* Albany, NY: SUNY Press.

Petronio, S. (2010). Communication privacy management theory: What do we know about family privacy regulation? *Journal of Family Theory & Review, 2,* 175–196.

Petronio, S., Jones, S. & Morr, M. C. (2003). Family privacy dilemmas: Managing communication boundaries within family groups. In L. R. Frey (Ed.), *Group communication in context: Studies of bona fide groups.* (pp. 23–55). Mahwah, NJ: LEA.

Peplau, L. A. & Cochran, S. D. (1981). Value orientations in the intimate relationships of gay men. *Journal of Homosexuality, 6,* 1–9.

PEW Research Center for the People and the Press. (2013, June 6). *In gay marriage debate, both supporters and opponents see legal recognition as "inevitable."* Retrieved from http://www.people-press.org/2013/06/06/in-gay-marriage-debate-both-supporters -and-opponents-see-legal-recognition-as-inevitable/.

Pinello, D. R. (2006). *America's struggle for same-sex marriage.* Cambridge: Cambridge University Press.

Porche, M. V. & Purvin, D. M. (2008). "Never in our lifetime": Legal marriage for same-sex couples in long-term relationships. *Family Relations, 57,* 144–159.

Porche, M. V., Purvin, D. M., & Waddell, J. M. (2005). *Tying the knot: The context of social change in Massachusetts.* Wellesley, MA: Wellesley Centers for Women.

Purcell, D. W. (1997). Current trends in same-sex marriage. In R. J. Cabaj & D. W. Purcell (Eds.), *On the road to same-sex marriage: A supportive guide to psychological, political and legal issues.* (pp. 29–40). San Francisco: Jossey-Bass Inc.

Ramos, C., Goldberg, N. G., & Badgett, M. V. L. (2009). *The effects of marriage equality in Massachusetts: A survey of the experiences and impact of marriage on same-sex couples.* Los Angeles, CA: The Williams Institute, UCLA.

Recheck, C., Elliott, S., & Umberson, D. (2009). Commitment without marriage: Union formation among long-term same-sex couples. *Journal of Family Issues, 30,* 738–756.

Regnerus, M. (2012). How different are the adult children of parents who have same-sex relationships? Findings from the new family structures study. *Social Science Research, 41,* 735–751.

Riggle, E. D. B, Rostosky, S. S., & Horne, S. G. (2009). Marriage amendments and lesbian, gay, and bisexual individuals in the 2006 election. *Sexuality Research and Social Policy, 6,* 80–89.

Riggle, E. D. B., Rostosky, S. S. & Prather, R. A. (2006). Advance planning by same-sex couples. *Journal of Family Issues, 27,* 758–776.

Riggle, E. D. B., Rostosky, S. S. & Reedy, C. S. (2005). Online surveys for BGLT research: Issues and techniques. *Journal of Homosexuality, 49,* 1–21.

Rolfe, A. & Peel, E. (2011). "It's a double-edged thing": The paradox of civil partnership and why some couples are choosing not to have one. *Feminism & Psychology, 21,* 317–335.

Rostosky, S. S., Korfhage, B. A., Duhigg, J. M., Stern, A. J., Bennett, L., & Riggle, E. D. B. (2004). Same-sex couples perceptions of family support: A consensual qualitative study. *Family Process, 43,* 43–57.

Rostosky, S. S., Riggle, E. D. B., Horne, S.G., Denton, F. N., & Huellemier, J. D. (2010). Sexual minorities' psychological reactions to the 2006 marriage amendments. *American Journal of Orthopsychiatry, 80,* 302–310.

Rostosky, S. S., Riggle, E. D. B., Dudley, M. G., & Wright, M. L. C. (2006). Commitment in same-sex relationships: A qualitative analysis of couples' conversations. *Journal of Homosexuality, 51,* 199–223.

Rostosky, S. S., Riggle, E. D. B, Horne, S. G., & Miller, A. D. (2009). Marriage amendments and psychological distress in lesbian, gay, and bisexual (LGB) adults. *Journal of Counseling Psychology, 56,* 56–66.

Rubin, D. & Lannutti, P. J. (2001). Frameworks for assessing inter-group contact as a tool for reducing prejudice. In V. H Milhouse, V. H., M. Asante & P.O. Nwosu (Eds.), *Transcultural realities: Interdisciplinary perspectives on cross-cultural relations.* (pp. 313–326). Thousand Oaks, CA: SAGE Publications.

Russell, G. M. (2000). *Voted out: The psychological consequences of anti-gay politics.* New York: New York University Press.

Russell, G. M. (2011). Motives of heterosexual allies in collective action for equality. *Journal of Social Issues, 67,* 376–393.

Rust, P. C. (1995). *Bisexuality and the challenge to lesbian politics: Sex, loyalty, and revolution.* New York: NYU Press.

Rust, P. C. R. (2000). Neutralizing the political threat of the marginal woman: Lesbians' beliefs about bisexual women. In P. C. R. Rust (Ed.), *Bisexuality in the United States: A social science reader.* (pp. 471–495). New York: Columbia University Press.

Rutter, V. & Schwartz, P. (2000). Gender, marriage, and diverse possibilities for cross-sex and same-sex pairs. In D. H. Demo, K. R. Allen, & M. A. Fine (Eds.), *Handbook of family diversity.* (pp. 59–81). New York: Oxford University Press.

Savin-Williams, R. C. (2001). *Mom, Dad, I'm gay.* Washington, D.C.: American Psychological Association.

Schecter, E., Tracy, A. J., Page, K. V., Luong, G. (2008). Shall we marry? Legal marriage as a commitment event in same-sex relationships. *Journal of Homosexuality, 54,* 400–422.

Scherrer, K. S. (2008). Coming to an asexual identity: Negotiation identity, negotiating desire. *Sexualities, 11,* 621–641.

Scherrer, K. S. (2010). What asexuality contributes to the same-sex marriage discussion. *Journal of Gay and Lesbian Social Sciences, 22,* 56–73.

Schulman, J., Gotta, G., & Green, R. (2012). Will marriage matter? Effects of marriage anticipated by same-sex couples. *Journal of Family Issues, 33,* 158–181.

Schulman, S. (1994). *My American history: Lesbian and gay life during the Regan/Bush years.* New York: Routledge.

Schulman, S. (2009). *Ties that bind: Familial homophobia and its consequences.* New York: New York Press.

Serewicz, M. C., & Canary, D. J. (2008). Assessments of disclosure from the in-laws: Links among disclosure topics, family privacy orientations, and relational quality. *Journal of Social and Personal Relationships, 25,* 333–357.

Sherkat, D. E., de Vries, K. M., & Creek, S. (2010). Race, religion, and opposition to same-sex marriage. *Social Science Quarterly, 91,* 80–98.

Slater, S. (1995). *The lesbian family life cycle.* New York: The Free Press.

Smart, C. (2007). Same-sex couples and marriage: Negotiating relational landscapes with families and friends. *The Sociological Review, 55,* 671–686.

Smith, R. B. & Brown, R. A. (1997). The impact of social support on gay male couples. *Journal of Homosexuality, 33,* 39–61.

South, S. J. (1992). For love or money? Sociodemographic determinants of expected benefits of marriage. In S. J. South & S. E. Tolnay (Eds.), *The changing American family: Sociological and demographic perspectives.* (pp. 171–194). Boulder, CO: Westview Press.

Sprecher, S. & Metts, S. (1999). Romantic beliefs: Their influence on relationships and patterns of change over time. *Journal of Social and Personal Relationships, 16,* 834–851.

Stearns, D. C. & Sabini, J. (1997). Dyadic adjustment and community involvement in same-sex couples. *Journal of Gay, Lesbian, and Bisexual Identity, 2,* 265–283.

Stiers, G. (1999). *From this day forward: Commitment, marriage, and family in lesbian and gay relationships.* New York: St. Martin's Press.

Strauss, A. & Corbin, J. (2008). *Basics of qualitative research, 3rd Ed: Techniques and procedures for developing grounded theory.* Thousand Oaks, CA: SAGE.

Streitmatter, R. (2008). *From "perverts" to "fab five": The media's changing depiction of gay men and lesbians.* New York: Routledge.

Surra, C. A., Hughes, D. K., Jacquet, S. E. (1999). The development of commitment to marriage: A phenomenological approach. In J. M. Adams & W. H. Jones (Eds.), *Handbook of interpersonal commitment and relationship stability: Perspectives on individual differences.* (pp. 125–148). Dordrecht, Netherlands: Kluwer Academic Publishers.

Surra, C. A. & Perlman, D. (2003). Introduction: The many faces of context. *Personal Relationships, 10,* 1350–4126.

Suter, E. A., Bergen, K. M., Daas, K. L., Durham, W. T. (2006). Lesbian couples' management of public-private dialectical tensions. *Journal of Social and Personal Relationships, 23,* 349–365.

Suter, E. A. & Daas, K. L. (2007). Negotiating heteronormativity dialectically: Lesbian couples' display of symbols in culture. *Western Journal of Communication, 71,* 177—195.

Taylor, J. K. (2007). Transgender identities and public policy in the United States: The relevance for public administration. *Administration & Society, 39,* 833—856.

Tracy, K. (2002). *Everyday talk: Building and reflecting identities.* New York: Guilford Press.

Travers, J. & Milgram, S. (1969). An experimental study in the small world problem. *Sociometry, 35,* 425—443.

United States v. Windsor. 570 U. S. _____. June 26, 2013.

Walters, S. D. (2001). *All the rage: The story of gay visibility in America.* Chicago: The University of Chicago Press.

Weston, K. (1991). *Families we choose: Lesbians, gays, kinship.* New York: Columbia University Press.

Wharton, G. & Philips, I. (Eds.) (2004). *I do, I don't: Queers on marriage.* San Francisco: Suspect Thoughts Press.

Woolwine, D. (2000). Community in gay male experience and moral discourse. *Journal of Homosexuality, 38,* 5—37.

Worth, H., Reid, A., & McMillan, K. (2002). Somewhere over the rainbow: Love, trust and monogamy in gay relationships. *Journal of Sociology, 38,* 237—253.

Yep, G. A., Lovaas, K. E., & Elia, J. P. (2003). A critical appraisal of assimilationist and radical ideologies underlying same-sex marriage in LGBT communities in the United States. *Journal of Homosexuality, 45,* 45—64.

Index